TRADITIONAL
BEADWORK

TRADITIONAL
BEADWORK

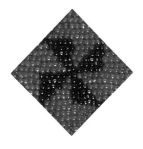

ELIZA McCLELLAND

ANAYA PUBLISHERS LTD
LONDON

To Michael, with all my love

First published in Great Britain in 1994
by Anaya Publishers Ltd, Strode House,
44-50 Osnaburgh Street, London NW1 3ND

Text copyright © Eliza McClelland 1994
Project photography and illustrations copyright
© Anaya Publishers Ltd 1994

Managing Editor: Jane Struthers
Design: Roger Daniels
Photography: Jon Stewart
Styling: Surfaces
Illustrations: Steve Dew and Delia Elliman
Picture Researcher: Adrian Bentley

British Library Cataloguing in Publication Data
McClelland, Eliza
Traditional Beadwork
I. Title
746.5

ISBN 1-85470-198-3

Typeset in Granjon by Bookworm Typesetting, Manchester
Colour reproduction by J. Film Process, Singapore
Printed and bound in Portugal by Printer Portuguesa Lda.

Note: The measurements given for the canvas and lining in each
project are intended only to be a guide. Each stitcher has a different
tension, which will alter the finished size of the canvas slightly, and
you may also want to adapt the patterns printed in this book.

Some US readers may be unfamiliar with some of the terms used in
this book, so it is suggested they refer to the glossary on page 112.

CONTENTS

WORKING WITH BEADS

Collecting beads and choosing the right bead for the job is huge fun. The basic rules of thumb are that anything goes and the more the merrier.

The first place to look for beads is in your own home: any loose beads at the bottom of your jewel box; any string of beads you haven't worn in years and which was always the wrong length; any glitter from a Christmas cracker or stocking that a visiting niece has pushed down the side of your sofa.

When you are sure you have scoured all existing supplies, move on to market stalls and outdoor sales. I have found many of those multi-stranded necklaces in such places and, when cut up, they provide handfuls of beads. I begrudge paying more than a few pennies for them. Occasionally, I have visited antique fairs and bought more expensively for specific projects – a sprinkling of old cut quartz can transform the look of a very large area of beading.

Of course, you can also buy from the commercial bead shops and suppliers. Lots of them do mail order. I first came across shop catalogues in theatre wardrobes and became as excited as a magpie by all that was on offer. Bead suppliers do not provide the myriad shades we are used to getting from yarn suppliers, but I have discovered lots of ways of gathering together more than enough shades.

First, the beads come in different finishes: translucent, opaque, pearlized, lustre, rainbow, silver-lined, metallic and matt – so there are eight shades for starters. Also, they come in different shapes (round, cut, bugle), each of which catches the light differently and provides contrast. And you can buy two or three different sizes of each shape. Sizes vary anyway, depending on the quality of bead and country of origin, but you will find, for example, that sizes nine, ten and eleven will all sit happily on a twelve-holes-to-inch canvas. The larger the bead, the less dense and lighter in colour it is.

Another trick is to stitch translucent beads with different coloured sewing threads. Imagine the same crystal beads stitched first with white, then pink, then grey cotton. Instantly you have three shades from one packet.

It is also possible to buy packets of beautifully graded matt beads, which I think are lovely; and mixed packets of multi-coloured and metallic 'sweepings' are a really good investment.

For some of my projects I wanted a really soft 'antiqued' look, so I asked Clare, the wardrobe supervisor at the Bristol Old Vic theatre, how costumes are broken down or aged. Through experiment and her advice I have come up with several easy methods:

● Pour some French enamel varnish (FEV) from a craft shop into a small plastic or glass container. Add your beads and leave them to soak for five minutes. Dredge them out and let them dry on newspaper.

● Pour some household bleach or dry-cleaning fluid into a small plastic or glass container. Soak your beads for five minutes. Pour the beads into an old tea strainer and rinse them well in hot running water.

● Bleach another batch of the same beads but leave them to soak for half an hour to break down the original colour still further.

● Leave metallic beads outside overnight in a drop of water to tarnish them.

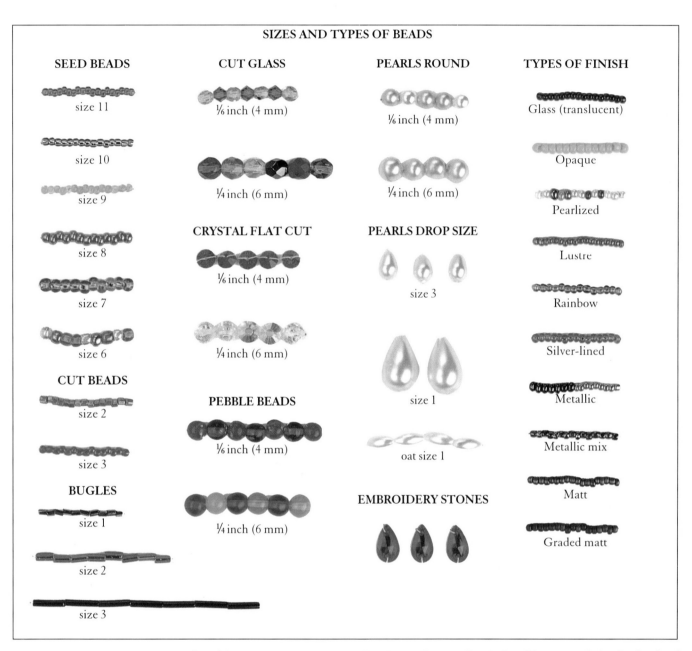

SIZES AND TYPES OF BEADS

SEED BEADS

size 11

size 10

size 9

size 8

size 7

size 6

CUT BEADS

size 2

size 3

BUGLES

size 1

size 2

size 3

CUT GLASS

⅙ inch (4 mm)

¼ inch (6 mm)

CRYSTAL FLAT CUT

⅙ inch (4 mm)

¼ inch (6 mm)

PEBBLE BEADS

⅙ inch (4 mm)

¼ inch (6 mm)

PEARLS ROUND

⅙ inch (4 mm)

¼ inch (6 mm)

PEARLS DROP SIZE

size 3

size 1

oat size 1

EMBROIDERY STONES

TYPES OF FINISH

Glass (translucent)

Opaque

Pearlized

Lustre

Rainbow

Silver-lined

Metallic

Metallic mix

Matt

Graded matt

In this way, everyone's collection of beads will be completely individual and you will be all set to create a unique piece of work. Use my charts as a guideline only. For example, where I have specified four reds (garnet, pearl, cut and rainbow), use any four that you like.

Be brave and start using billions of colours. It is easy to do this physically as you do not have to keep starting and ending yarns as you would with needlepoint. Using a different bead for each stitch will not result in the back of your work resembling coconut matting which has been put through a hot wash. Experiment by dropping in an unexpected colour – say a turquoise among silver, or a bronze among green. You will see that it doesn't scream at you but just softly enriches the whole. It is truly impossible to go wrong as all beads stitched in any order are beautiful. Whatever happens, you can be sure of creating something lovely that will last forever.

TILE CHAIR SEAT

Home is where it all started. We had bought a bargain second-hand chair and it needed a cushion. I wanted one to fit it exactly and to go with the warm, jolly colours in our hall. I sat on the stairs gazing vacantly at the sunlight spilling on to the glazed Victorian floor tiles, dejectedly realizing that anything I produced would look like clutter against them. Suddenly, I had it! I sat down with a piece of tracing paper, and drew round the tiles' geometric pattern. It was easy to transfer this on to canvas (see page 106), and so I was off. I stitched around the edge of each 'tile' first, using long stitch over two threads, and worked inwards so that each tile still looked like an individual part of the whole. But I knew I was still missing the deep glow which makes our hall so welcoming. Edging the cushion with big glass beads was the answer.

I have since used the idea of beaded edgings on plain silk cushions and it never fails to add unusual glamour and twinkle. I have charted the shape I actually made, but it would be very easy to add or subtract a strip of tiles. Better still, get out your tracing paper and draw around your own hall tiles, your sofa fabric, your spare room curtains…the world is your oyster.

Materials
12-holes-to-inch single thread canvas, measuring 21 inches square (52.5 cm square)
Beads and yarns (see below)
Beading needle
Size 18 tapestry needle
Sewing needle
Velvet for backing, measuring 21 inches square (52.5 cm square)
Button thread
Cushion pad

To work
The bulk of the cushion is worked in straight or diagonal stitches over two threads of canvas. The angles of these stitches are clearly marked on the chart, but be careful to work them in an order which produces the shape of the tiles. Start with the black outline of the centre square and build outwards from there.

The squares
Stitch around the perimeter, then work in ever decreasing circles to the centre.

The triangles
Work from point A up to B, then down to C. Then work from C up to B, then down to A.

The arrows
Keep the shape of the 'arrowhead' as you work from side to side.

The diamonds
Work straight across.

The red and gold side squares are worked in tent stitch and the central motif is in random long stitch. As you can see from the list of yarns, each colour has 2–4 shades listed. The Paterna yarn splits into three threads, but the crewel wool is just one thread. Select your own mixture of threads (use three threads in one needle), varying it each time so the colours blend into each other and the direction of your stitching shows up clearly.

To make up
Stretch your finished canvas. Trim it to shape, leaving a ½-inch (12-mm) seam allowance all round. Using this as a pattern, cut out the silk backing to the same shape. With right sides together, stitch the backing velvet to the canvas

The Tile Chair Seat in situ in our hall.

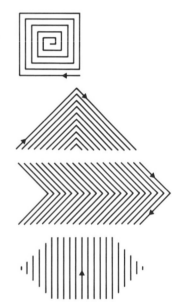

along three sides. Slip in the cushion pad. Sew up the fourth edge.

The beaded edge
Collect about 150 beads. I used only the colours already in the project (jet, red, sapphire, amber, brown and clear), but chose as many different shapes and sizes as I could find. The sizes range from ¼ inch (5 mm) to ⅝ inch (14 mm), the sort usually used for necklaces. Broken necklaces are the best source of unusual and cheap beads, but craft shops hold wide ranges. Using button thread, stitch on the first bead, then secure it with a second stitch as you would a button. Move on to the next bead until your edge is complete.

Only half this design has been printed. Stitch the other half as a mirror image.

Yarns *No. of skeins*

Paterna 220 black	1

Paterna 552 ice blue	1
Paterna 554 ice blue	1
Paterna 502 federal blue	1
Paterna 503 federal blue	1

Paterna 263 white/cream	5

Paterna 411 earth brown	1
Paterna 470 toast brown	2
Paterna 471 toast brown	2
Paterna 472 toast brown	2

Appleton's crewel 901	3
Appleton's crewel 912	3
Appleton's crewel 913	2

Paterna 442 golden brown	3
Paterna 733 honey gold	1
Appleton's crewel 901	2

Appleton's crewel 954	2
Appleton's crewel 913	2
Appleton's crewel 914	2

Paterna 861 copper	1
Paterna 401 fawn brown	1

DMC 783 coton perlé no 3	1
DMC 420 stranded cotton	1
DMC 676 stranded cotton	1

Note: Paterna yarns are sold as Paternayan in the U.S.

Beads
A mixture of the colours already used in the project – jet, red, sapphire, amber, brown and clear – in sizes ranging from ¼ inch (6 mm) to ⅝ inch (14 mm). Use about 150 beads in all.

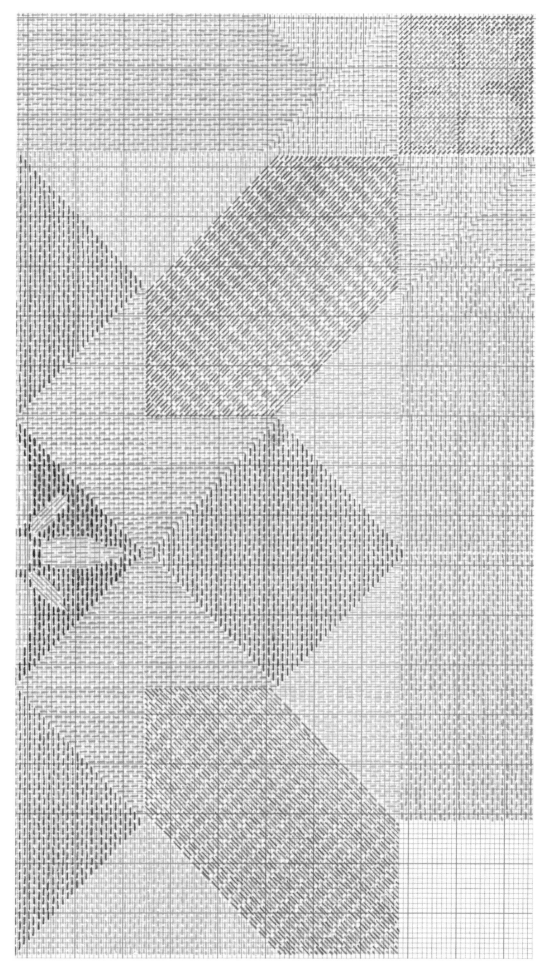

STAINED GLASS MAT

Facing page: The Stained Glass Mat, showing clearly how many different beads are included. *Below:* The exterior of the Five Sisters Window at York Minster. *Below right:* The Five Sisters Window from inside the cathedral. The design of the mat is a detail from the bottom of the left lancet.

As the cookie happens to crumble, I have worked in York, at the Theatre Royal, on lots of occasions. I love it there. In summer I walk to work early, at about six, so I can listen to all the street musicians playing in the Shambles, sniff the smell of warm scones floating out into the evening air from Betty's Tearooms and catch the end of the market for some fruit for the dressing room.

I regularly stroll through York Minster because it is wonderful. In the north wall of the north transept is the Five Sisters Window, shining with a grey northern light. It is patterned with geometric shapes on a background of grey foliage. This is the healing geum plant. There is a legend that the pat-terns came from five pieces of embroi-dery stitched by five maiden sisters, a legend which Charles Dickens embroi-ders further in *Nicholas Nickleby*.

I thought it would be good to try to put the window back on canvas, and tried to reproduce the grisaille glass by using all the lovely old crystal beads that I had. I used an old amber neck-lace, bought some blue Bohemian quartz and soaked the rose and lime beads in some French enamel varnish (FEV). This project taught me, more than any other, that the more odd, con-trasting beads you slip in, the richer the whole piece becomes. Buy a bag of mixed 'sweepings', have a go at break-ing down some beads and you'll be up and running.

Materials

12-holes-to-inch double-thread
    canvas, measuring 20 inches square
    (50 cm square)
Beads and yarns (see below)
Beading needle
Size 18 tapestry needle
Sewing needle
Polyester sewing cotton
Silk for backing, measuring 20 inches
    square (50 cm square)

To work

Start by working the grey outline of the
leading in tent stitch. Then bead each
pane separately, starting from the blue
centre. I beaded the diamond panes
using many different shades of grey,
beige, white and pink cotton threads.

To make up

Stretch your finished canvas. Trim it to
shape, leaving a ½-inch (12-mm) seam
allowance all round. Using this as a
pattern, cut out the silk backing to the
same shape. With right sides together,
hand-sew the silk lining to the edge of
the canvas, leaving a small gap in one
side. Trim the edges of the fabric and
canvas. Turn right sides out. Slip-stitch
the gap. Press with a cool iron on the
wrong side.

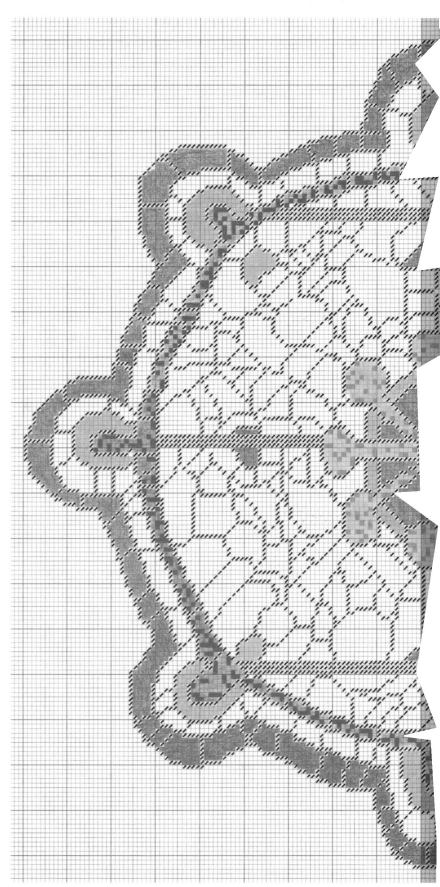

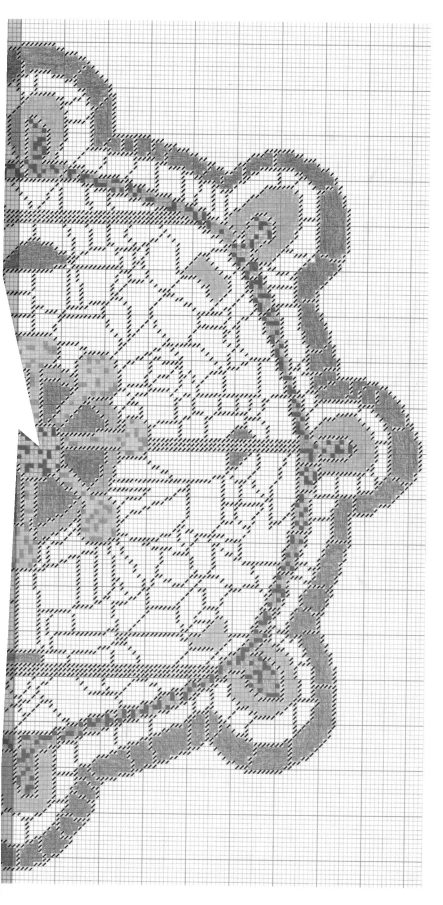

Yarns
No. of skeins

✏ DMC 413 coton perlé no 3   3

Beads
No. of beads

▨	Light sapphire crystal glass (⅛ inch/4 mm)	500
▨	Sapphire crystal glass (⅛ inch/4 mm)	100
▨	Lime (size 10)	1 pkt
▨	Emerald (size 10)	1 pkt
	Green metallic (size 10)	1 pkt
▨	Deep rose cut (size 3)	2 pkts
▨	Amber cut (size 3)	1 pkt

The diamond colours
Collect as many different diamond, crystal and silvery beads as you can. Use old beads or age new ones (see page 6). Sizes 7-11 would be fine in round, cut or bugle shapes. You will need approximately ten packets, depending on the number of extra incidental colours you use.

'Sweepings'
These are dotted through your crystal panels at random. You only need a scant few of each colour so use up any leftovers you have, or buy a mixed packet. Start with kingfisher blue, purple, amber, green and metallic mix and experiment from there.

WREN AND SPIDER CUSHION

This pesky little wren with his spider comes from one of the small diamond panes in the Zouche Chapel, a quiet side chapel in York Minster. Each of the tiny 15th-century panes has a different picture: there is an astonished eagle; a one-man band; a chorus line of monkeys and a sitting duck. They are all at eye level and easy to see. I chose the wren as I was doing a show about tap dancing at the time and I found that his shuffle-hop-step cheered me on with mine.

All the beads in this project started life bright and glitzy and new. I had used up every single one of my old beads on the grisaille York Minster window (see pages 12-15) so I had to break down or age ordinary beads with household bleach. I was pleased with the way the crystalline beads broke down. I kept the sizes of the beads regular here, which gives a humbler look than the mighty grisaille, and I made sure I filled the cushion tightly so it looks chubby. Stained glass is the perfect subject for beadwork. Why not do your own favourite piece?

Left: The wren and spider pane in the Zouche Chapel at York Minster. *Facing page:* My fat wren on my Wren and Spider Cushion.

Materials

12-holes-to-inch double-thread
   canvas, measuring 13 inches square
   (32.5 cm square)
Beading needle
Size 18 tapestry needle
Sewing needle
Beads and yarns (see below)
Polyester sewing cotton
Velvet for cushion front and for
   backing, 2 pieces each measuring
   13 inches square
   (32.5 cm square)
1¼ yards (1 metre) fine cord
1¾ yards (1½ metres) edging cord
Cushion pad

To work

Start by beading the wren and spider's web, then bead the background and side lights. Bead the side lights randomly with blue beads – I simply made sure that each one had a different dominant shade. Make up your mixture before you start each panel – two pinches of dominant blue, one pinch of each of any others – then just stitch on the beads as they come. Use tent stitch for the black borders.

To make up

Stretch your finished work. Insert it into one piece of velvet (see page 106) and cover any signs of stitching with the fine cord. Right sides together, stitch the backing velvet to the front piece on three sides. Insert the cushion pad. Sew up the fourth side. Edge with cord and sew the ends up neatly.

Yarn	*No. of skeins*
DMC 310 coton perlé no 3	2

Beads		*No. of beads*
	Brown (size 10)	1 pkt
	Purple (size 10)	1 pkt
	Black (size 10)	1 pkt
	Brown crystal (size 10)	1 pkt
	Brown metallic (size 10)	1 pkt
	Amber cut (size 3)	1 pkt
	Emerald (size 10)	1 pkt
	Lime (size 10)	1 pkt

Blues

Random selection of pale blues, royal blue and turquoises. Sizes 9-11 would be fine in round, cut or bugle shapes; or buy two packets of graded blues.

Diamonds

The background glass is all silver and crystal colours, which are then broken down. You will need approximately two packets, but a huge mixture is best. One or two limes, purples and ambers have also crept into my cushion.

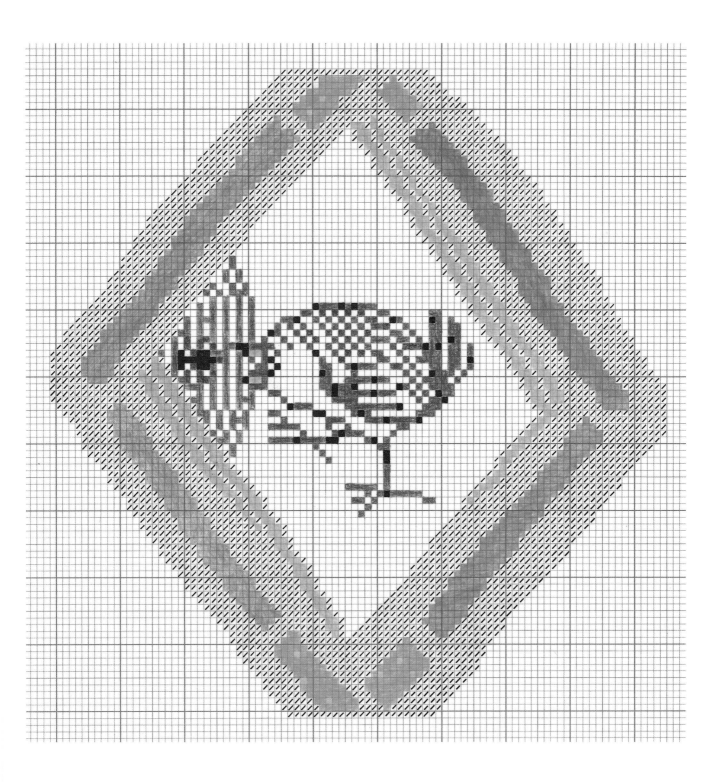

PATCHWORK NIGHTDRESS CASE

Shortly after we moved house, I did a long season at the Haymarket Theatre in Leicester. At that point our bedroom furnishings consisted of a bed, a dressmaker's dummy and a Mickey Mouse phone. I decided to make us a quilt with some of the galaxy of fabric leftovers in the theatre wardrobe. The quilt began, suitably, with bits of Joseph's well-worn Dreamcoat and then I stitched on every sequin, button or ribbon I could scavenge, resulting in a vastly jolly but eccentric cover. When I saw this mid-western Amish quilt in America, I wished I had been just a touch more restrained.

The pinwheel pattern is totally simple but alive. Amish women abhorred showy appliqué but used elaborate quilting stitch patterns to join their patchwork to the wool lining and calico backing. I thought the perfect way to reproduce the famous Amish jewel colours against a dark background would be in beads, but I have used a mixture of textured stitches in the charcoal squares to suggest the quilting patterns. Alternatively, you could bead these dark squares in jet. Substitute any colours you like in the pinwheel squares, but try to have at least two tones per colour. Any leftovers or packets of graded beads are ideal for this project. The distinctly American patchwork is a lovely contribution to a secure and happy family hearth. Make one for yours.

Facing page: My nightie case, showing the classic jewel colours of Amish design. *Right:* A typical Amish quilt showing the beautiful stitch patterns.

Yarns

No. of skeins

// Mosaic stitch ⎫
⌐ Bullion knots ⎬ Use a random mix of DMC 413 coton perlé no 3 (3 skeins), DMC 413 stranded cotton (6 skeins) and DMC 413 coton perlé no 5 (5 skeins)
× Cross stitch ⎭

Beads

Reds

Flame (size 11) 1 pkt

Deep red (size 9) 1 pkt

Red silver-lined (size 11) 1 pkt

Red rainbow (size 9) 1 pkt

Oranges

Orange cut (size 3) 1 pkt

Orange silver-lined (size 11) 1 pkt

Blues

Turquoise graded (size 9) 1 pkt

Turquoise opaque (size 10) 1 pkt

Pale blue cut (size 3) 1 pkt

Mercury (size 11) 1 pkt

Royal blue (size 10) 1 pkt

Matt Air Force blue (size 10) 1 pkt

Browns

Brown (size 10) 1 pkt

Mocha matt (size 10) 1 pkt

Yellows

Amber graded (size 9) 1 pkt

Amber cut (size 3) 1 pkt

Yellow graded (size 9) 1 pkt

Gold silver-lined (size 11) 1 pkt

Metallic mixture cut(size 3) 1 pkt

Pinks

Soft pink (size 10) 1 pkt

Claret (size 11) 1 pkt

Rose cut (size 3) 1 pkt

Purples

Matt purple graded (size 10) 1 pkt

Purple seed (size 10) 1 pkt

Purple rainbow (size 9) 1 pkt

Greens

Lime green glass seed (size 10) 1pkt

Metallic green cut (size 3) 1 pkt

Matt bottle green glass (size 9) 1 pkt

Bottle green glass seed (size 9)1 pkt

Emerald seed (size 10) 1 pkt

Emerald cut (size 3) 1 pkt

Matt olive seed (size 10) 1 pkt

Kingfisher cut (size 3) 1 pkt

Materials

12-holes-to-inch double-thread
  canvas, measuring approximately
  14 x 12 inches (35 x 30 cm)
Beads and yarns (see page 22)
Size 18 tapestry needle
Beading needle
Sewing needle
Polyester sewing cotton
Taffeta fabric for case
Lightweight padding

To work

Start by stitching all the quilted charcoal patches. These consist of a central
panel of mosaic stitch (see page 108)
surrounded by forty small bullion
knots (see page 108). The position of
the base thread of the knots is marked
on the chart. The corners of these
squares are cross-stitched. Use the
coton perlé weights and stranded cotton at random to create different tex-
tures, but the bullion knots are best
'wrapped' with coton perlé no 5. Now
bead each pinwheel square and the red
border.

To make up

Stretch your finished canvas.

Measure your stretched work and
cut three pieces of fabric as shown
below. Each one is 2 inches (5 cm)
wide, which includes a ½-inch (12-
mm) seam allowance on each of the
four sides.

Pin these pieces to the canvas as
shown below and hand-stitch them
in place, joining the mitred corners.
Cut a long piece of fabric as shown,
again with a ½-inch (12-mm) seam
allowance on each side.

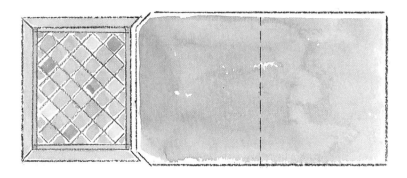

Stitch this piece of fabric in place
along the canvas. Cut the interfacing to
the size of the whole piece and tack in
place. With right sides together,
machine-stitch the lining in place, leaving a 6-inch (15-cm) gap. Turn right
sides out and hand-stitch the gap. Fold
up the case and stitch up the top and
bottom seams of the pocket.

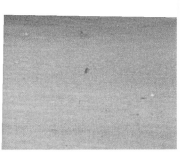

An Amish family at work in
Pennsylvania.

25

DICKENS BOOKMARK

Dickens has always been very good to actors. He gave a first edition copy of *Nicholas Nickleby* to his friend, the actor Macready. The book is on display in Dickens House in London. An accompanying letter reads '…the red represents my blushes at its gorgeous dress, the gildings all those bright professions which I do not make to you, and the book itself my whole heart for twenty months.'

I visited Dickens House when I was rehearsing five different parts in *Hard Times*. All Dickens' characters are gifts to play, being so vibrant and quirky, and, once discovered, they tend to live with you always. Our Christmases never pass without Tiny Tim's 'Absent Friends' being toasted, and I remember my father as a brilliant Rogue Riderhood on television before we even possessed one.

Dickens himself was not slow in coming forward. His tours of dramatic readings from his books were hugely successful in the last twelve years of his life. His lectern and reading copies are on display at the house, all marked up with jolly reminders to 'slap the desk' or 'kiss hand'. One wonders if he was a terrible old ham storming his way across America, but I felt I could do a lot worse than borrow some of his panache to see me through my *Hard Times*. I decided to stitch up a bookmark. It would be simple, dramatic, Christmassy and immediate. This is the easiest project in the book and could even be attempted by a nimble-fingered child. I think it is worth using two different red yarns because they really do add the depth of Moroccan leather to the finish. And don't stint on the tassel lengths.

Facing page: The bookmark and Macready's copy of *Nicholas Nickleby* photographed at Dickens House, Doughty Street, London. The china ornament always sat on Dickens' desk.
Below: My father on the front of the *Radio Times* – Richard Leech as Rogue Riderhood in *Our Mutual Friend*.

Above: Charles Dickens as himself.

Materials

10-holes-to-inch double-thread
   canvas, measuring 15 inches square
   (37.5 cm square) because this
   design is worked on the bias
Beading needle
Size 18 tapestry needle
Darning needle
Sewing needle
Beads and yarns (see below)
Polyester sewing cotton
Silk backing fabric, measuring
   15 inches square
   (37.5 cm square)

To work

Working with your canvas on the bias
(as in the chart), start by stitching on
the gold beads. Fill in the red beads
(omitting the edging ones) and then
work the red cross stitch. I worked the
whole area in half the cross stitch with
one shade of red and then reworked it
from the opposite direction in a slightly darker shade to complete the cross
stitch. This adds depth and richness.

To make up

Gently press your finished canvas and
carefully trim to size, then cut the silk
backing to the right size. Stitch on the
silk backing, turning under the raw
edges all the way round. You will still
have a bare hole of canvas all round the
edge of the work but this will be filled.
To make the tassels: cut 6-inch (15-
cm) lengths of your two shades of red
yarn and a gold metallic thread.
Thread one of each of these through a
darning needle (three different threads
in one needle) and draw through a
bare hole on the short edge of the work.
Knot the threads as you would a lug-
gage label. When you have completed
the tassels, stitch red beads into the
bare holes on the long edges of the
book mark.

Yarns		No. of skeins
![red]	DMC 666 coton perlé no 3	2
![dark red]	DMC 321 coton perlé no 3	2
	Gold metallic thread 13 yards (12 metres)	

Beads		No. of beads
![gold]	Gold (size 8)	1 pkt
![red bead]	Red (size 10)	1 pkt

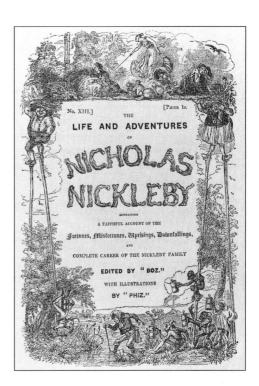

Above: The painting *Dickens' Dream*,
showing Charles Dickens surrounded by
characters from his books. *Top right:* The
cover of the first magazine installment of
Nicholas Nickleby. Right: An illustration of
one of the main characters from the novel,
the ghastly Wackford Squeers, who ran the
school Dotheboys Hall.

PETER PAN COLLAR

The bronze statue of Peter Pan in London's Kensington Gardens is found at the second gate to the left past Marble Arch. Peter himself lives second to the right and then straight on till morning.

The little boy who never grew up and tried to stick his shadow on with soap has a wonderful magic. The show has been performed at Christmas in Britain nearly every year since it was written in 1904. I used to love it when I was a child. Apparently, the very first night ever had to be postponed because of the tricky machinery, but the best effect was the simplest: Tinkerbell. A hand-held mirror catches a beam of spotlight and reflects it on

the stage, creating Tinkerbell. That naughty sprite flits and glitters through the evening and I always feel she is never far from the statue, dancing on the bronze with her pals.

My sister's godfather made his first professional appearance as Slightly in the show, so it seemed fitting to make a Peter Pan collar for my sister's daughter, Daisy. The Peter Pan shape, which lies flat and follows the line of the shoulder, is a pretty one and, as it is made in two pieces, it can be attached to all sorts of party dresses. I would recommend sewing for this as soap is not reliable. I loved working with the soft magical glitter of the bronzes and metallics for a change.

Materials

12-holes-to-inch double-thread
  canvas, 2 pieces each measuring
  15 inches square
  (37.5 cm square)
Beading needle
Size 18 tapestry needle
Sewing needle
Beads and yarns (see below)
Polyester sewing cotton
Silk backing fabric, 2 pieces each
  measuring 15 inches square
  (37.5 cm square)

To work

Start by beading an outline for each animal. Then bead specific areas that need clear demarcation: eyes, ears, tails, arms, legs, noses, beaks, throats, breasts. Fill in the rest either according to the chart or randomly as you please. Just make sure that one overall metallic colour is dominant for each animal: grey for the mouse; blue for the bird; brown for the squirrel and rabbits. Bead the pan pipes and then fill in the background with tent stitch. Make the other side as the mirror image.

My niece, Daisy Bell, standing beside the Peter Pan statue in Kensington Gardens, London. The statue was carved by Sir George Frampton.

To make up

Stretch your finished canvases. Trim them to shape, leaving a ½-inch (12-cm) seam allowance all the way round. Using them as patterns, cut out the silk backing pieces. With right sides together, stitch each canvas to its backing piece, leaving a small gap. Turn right sides out and stitch up the gaps. I stitched on seven oat pearls to each of the front edges to make a pretty finish. As the collar is in two pieces, it will sit well round the neck of many different party dresses.

Far left: Noël Coward in 1913 as Slightly, one of the Lost Boys. *Left:* Peter Pan dancing with his shadow. *Above:* Julia Lockwood as Peter Pan in the show in December 1963. *Right:* The author of *Peter Pan*, Sir J. M. Barrie, shown on a cigarette card.

SIR J. M. BARRIE, Bart.

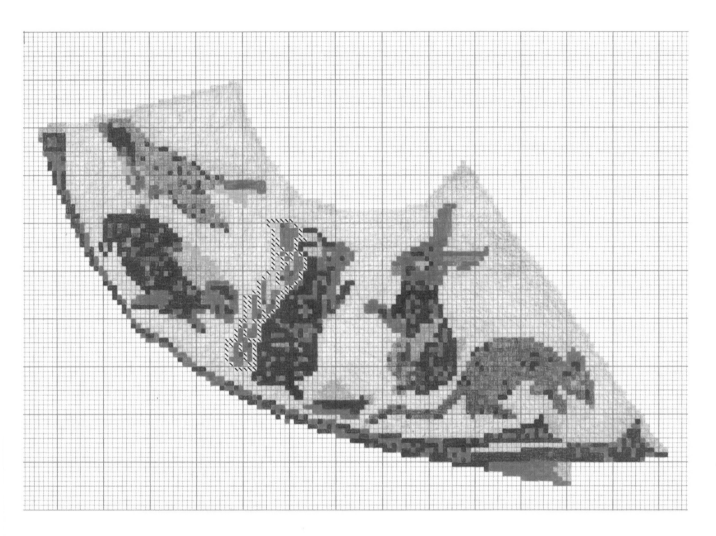

Yarn   *No. of skeins*

DMC 828 coton perlé no 3   5

Beads   *No. of beads*

Grey metallic (size 10)   1 pkt

Brown metallic (size 10)   2 pkts

Blue metallic (size 10)   1 pkt

Green metallic (size 10)   1 pkt

Bronze (size 10)   2 pkts

Gold (size 8)   1 pkt

Grey metallic (size 8)   1 pkt

Brown glass (size 10)   1 pkt

Brown crystal (size 10)   1 pkt

Bronze (size 9)   1 pkt

Bronze cut (size 3)   1 pkt

Pink metallic (size 3)   1 pkt

\ Bronze bugle
(size 1)   1 pkt

Oat pearls (size 1) 14 beads for edging

33

JAPANESE MAKE-UP BOX

My make-up box used to be a shoe-box tied with a dance elastic. Inside, it looked as if a bomb had exploded. It contained a zillion lipsticks in every shade from Eva Braun's deep matt stain to Mlle Jolibonbon's surprise pink. There was a shower of hairpins, some red and some white, which went part-way to securing Lady Fanciful's powdered wig. There was foundation: blue for the Jumbly Girl, ivory for anything by Mr Chekhov and flesh for anything by Mr Cooney. There were two opened packets of Fisherman's Friends and one of jelly teddies; a rat-tail comb; three mascaras; my eyeshadow box from Saks Fifth Avenue, some pebbles from Bourne-mouth and fifteen paintbrushes, big and small. It was time to turn over a new leaf.

The Japanese Noh tradition is the oldest extant professional theatre and they Noh all about make-up and masks. We have lots of books at home about Japan as, curiously, Michael studied Japanese at Cambridge, so I easily found the watercolour of old Segawa Tomisaburo and his bee-stung lips. Noh actors all come from an hereditary line of performers and are trained early in the ways of the slow-moving dance dramas. The soloist wears many traditional masks during the show and represents heroes, old men, young women, demons, deities and madmen at the drop of a hat. His protagonist has no mask, just a beauti-fully painted, impassive face.

I used lots of old beads for this pro-ject. Black and white are the easiest to find in junk shops but, somehow, you must gather three different shades of white for the face. I used different coloured threads here too. The collar is beaded with the same white beads but the 'inside' of it seems more shaded because I used grey thread. The black bugles for his hair are worth getting because they suggest the texture so well. If you want a bigger box, cover another layer of vegetable steamer.

Materials
12-holes-to-inch double-thread
   canvas, measuring approximately
   13 inches square
   (32.5 cm square)
Beads and yarns (see below)
Size 18 tapestry needle
Beading needle
Sewing needle
Polyester sewing cotton
Vegetable steamer (top and two layers)
⅝ yard (½ metre) lightweight padding
Fabric to cover the sides and bottom of
   the steamer
1½ yards (1.4 metres) thick piping

Facing page: The Japanese Make-up Box standing ready for use in my dressing room. *Below:* A Kabuki actor putting on his make-up.

35

To work

Start by beading the eyes and nose and work outwards from there. When beading the wig, don't follow the grid provided by your canvas. Instead, start with a base line of bugle beads above the ears, then sew the next line flush to this, and so on, working upwards. Likewise, the pebble beads of the lapel are bigger than the canvas and should be stitched flush to each other. The 'comb' effect is made by long stitches, as shown on the chart. Finish by stitching the background in tent stitch.

To make up

Stretch your finished canvas. Cut the lightweight padding to the exact size of the top and edges of the steamer. Attach the padding to the steamer with fabric glue or double-sided tape. Hand-stitch thick piping round the tapestry. Cut a strip of covering fabric on the bias, making it 1½ inches (38 millimetres) wider than the side of the steamer. Join the short sides to form a circle. Hand-stitch this on to the piped edge of the canvas, right sides together. Slide this over the top of the steamer, pull taut and secure it in place with fabric glue. Make two more circlets of covering fabric and attach them with glue to the top and bottom of the next two layers.

Below: A scene from a show performed in London in 1991 by the Umewaka Kennokai Noh Theatre. *Facing page:* The original watercolour of Segawa Tomisaburo by Toshusai Sharaku, which gave me the idea for the Make-up Box.

Yarns

No. of skeins

/ DMC 801 coton perlé no 3   1

▦ DMC 115 mouliné special
25 (used double)   8

Beads

No. of beads

▦ Black opaque (size 10)   2

▦ Grey (size 10)   1 pkt

▦ Grey metallic (size 10)   1 pkt

▦ Green metallic (size 10)   1 pkt

▦ Red (size 10)   3

▦ Garnet (size 11)   3

3 shades of white
beads (size 10)   1 pkt of each

▦ Frosted white cut (size 3)   1 pkt

▦ Pink metallic cut (size 3)   1 pkt

▦ Rose cut (size 3)   1 pkt

▦ Plum (size 11)   1 pkt

▦ Pink lustre (size 10)   1 pkt

○ Grey pebble ($\frac{1}{6}$ inch/4 mm)   60

● Brown pebble ($\frac{1}{6}$ inch/4 mm)   1

◉ Amber pebble ($\frac{1}{6}$ inch/4 mm)   2

▦ Amber (size 9)   1 pkt

▦ Bronze metallic (size 10)   1 pkt

▦ Copper metallic (size 10)   1 pkt

▦ Brown (size 10)   1 pkt

/ Amber bugle (size 1)   1 pkt

/// Black bugles (size 1,
size 2, size 3)   1 pkt of each

GOLDEN ROSE CUSHION

I have a strangely clear memory of the first time I went to the theatre. It was my fourth birthday and I was taken to a box at the Theatre Royal in London's Drury Lane to see *My Fair Lady*. I was riveted by the glamour of the liveried footmen front of house, the extraordinary black and white of the Ascot costumes designed by Cecil Beaton and the image of Eliza with her smutty face, damp boots and sweet violets. All through my babyhood I insisted on going to fancy-dress parties as that girl. So when I saw this beautiful soft watercolour by Beaton at Chartwell in Kent, I knew I would love to have a bit of him in my house. It is one of twenty-nine illustrations of different golden rose varieties that were planted to make the beautiful walk in the garden at Chartwell, the home of Sir Winston Churchill. Each rose was painted by a clever artist of the day. And all this was organized by the Churchill children to celebrate darling Clementine and Winston's golden wedding anniversary. It is a lovely romantic thought.

I stitched my boxed cushion in watery golden colours, gave it a background of Ascot lavender grey and spangled it with a broad band of 'coffee sugar' beads. Pinch the idea to surround any tapestry of your own. Collect as many different beads in your colour spectrum as you can find, pour them all into a bowl and mix well. You will soon find yourself covering your canvas at a gallop.

Above: The Golden Rose Walk at Chartwell in Kent.

Right: The Golden Rose Cushion.

Materials

12-holes-to-inch double-thread
    canvas, measuring approximately
    14 inches square
    (35 cm square)
Beading needle
Size 18 tapestry needle
Sewing needle
Beads and yarns (see below)
Polyester sewing cotton
Silk backing fabric, measuring
    approximately 14 inches square
    (35 cm square) plus one piece
    2 inches (5 cm) wide × 41 inches
    (103.5 cm) long
3¼ yards (3 metres) thick edging cord
Cushion pad

To work

Starting from the centre, work the rose
design and complete the background
silk. Mix all your beads in a bowl and
stitch them randomly to make a border
twelve rows deep.

To make up

Stretch your finished canvas. Using
this as a pattern (but adding a
½-inch/12-mm seam allowance) cut
out the cushion back from the silk.
Also, cut a side piece 2 inches (5 cm)
wide by 41 inches (103.5 cm) long.
With the right sides together, stitch this
long piece round your canvas. Sew up
the two short sides. Then stitch three
sides of the back piece to this. Turn
right sides out and insert your cushion
pad. Stitch up the fourth side. Cover
the seams with two lengths of edging
cord.

Yarns

DMC stranded cotton, or equivalent
silks (used double)

No. of skeins

	DMC 444	2
	DMC 307	2
	DMC 445	2
	DMC 746	2
	DMC 890	1
	DMC 367	1
	DMC 368	1
	DMC 369	1
	DMC 839	1
	DMC 841	1
	DMC 3743	10

Beads

Choose a jolly mixture of seed beads in
yellows, purples and crystal. I used:

	Bright yellow (size 8)	1 pkt
	Primrose pearl (size 10)	1 pkt
	Purple (size 10)	1 pkt
	Pink (size 10)	1 pkt
	Crystal (size 7)	1 pkt
	Amber cut (size 2)	1 pkt
	Purple cut (size 2)	1 pkt
	Mauve cut (size 2)	1 pkt

Top: Beaton's watercolour of
the golden rose 'Phyllis Gold'
which is included in the
commemorative book on
display at Chartwell. *Above:*
Beaton with one of his Ascot
designs.

PURUKPARLI'S SUNGLASSES CASE

I once spent Christmas at Leeds' City Varieties theatre, squeezed into the smallest dressing room in the world with Debra, an Australian soap actress who was playing the Blue Fairy, and Laurie, who was chameleon-like as the Alien from Alwoodly, the Stiltwalker and the Leader of the show-stopping Shrimp Ballet. I was Ginger the Cat and we were telling the story of *Pinocchio*. Laurie and I gossiped to Debra about warm leather jackets, Stratford-upon-Avon and Liberty's bedlinen department. She told us of the fab beach view from her balcony, the Sydney Opera House and the legends and dreams incorporated in Aboriginal art. So later, when an exhibition came over to the Hayward Gallery in London, I hightailed down there to have a look.

Aboriginal art is mostly pointillistic and immediately beadable. The colours are natural as the artists use natural pigments, often on bark, and add stones, feathers, bones, shells and seeds. And they all tell a story. This one tells of Purukparli's son who is neglected by his adulterous mum, Bima, and dies. Bima's lover, Tapara, is shown at the bottom of the picture in a boat holding the sticks with which he fought Purukparli. Purukparli does not allow Tapara to try to bring his son back to life but, instead, wraps him in paperbark and carries him out to sea.

Facing page: The sunglasses case.
Below: An Aboriginal painting on bark.

The central horizontal bar represents the body and the two silver verticals above it are Purukparli's arms cradling his son. Above these are his footprints walking out to sea, topped by the circular yellow and red whirlpool in which they drowned. The moon at the top is the cheer, symbolizing being reborn afresh the next night.

Don't feel you have to track down the exact beads I used for this project. A goodly selection of reds, metallics, browns and greys will work naturally. The smaller mesh of the canvas used results in the beads lying tightly together and forming a good guard for your sunglasses.

Materials
14-holes-to-inch double-thread
    canvas, 2 pieces measuring
    approximately 12 x 7½ inches
    (30 x 19 cm)
Beading needle
Size 18 tapestry needle
Sewing needle
Beads and yarns (see below)
Soft fabric glasses case
Polyester sewing cotton

To work
Following the chart, stitch on the gold metallic beads (size 10). This will give you a framework for the shapes, so it will be easy to complete them with the rows and middles of silver, red and yellow. Next, bead the rows dividing up the background and then complete the grey, brown and gold areas. Stitch the 'bark' bottom and the 'moonlight' shining through in your brown and silver yarns, using tent stitch.

To make up
Stretch your two pieces of finished canvas. Turn under the edges and hand-stitch them on to the glasses case.

The bark painting
The Death of Purukparli
by Marruwani.

Yarns	No. of skeins
DMC 938 coton perlé no 3	1
Thick silver metallic yarn	1

Beads	No. of beads
Gold metallic (size 10)	1 pkt
Silver metallic cut (size 3)	1 pkt
4 reds (sizes 10-11): ruby, opaque, metallic, wine	1 pkt of each

2 yellows (sizes 10-11): peach pearl, gold silver-lined	1 pkt of each
Brown (size 10)	1 pkt
Pewter metallic (size 10)	1 pkt
2 browns (sizes 10-11): mocha matt, copper metallic	1 pkt of each
2 greys (sizes 10-11): grey pearl, graded matt	1 pkt of each
3 golds (sizes 10-11): gold metallic, gold silver-lined as above, plus warm metallic mix	1 pkt of each

CROWN JEWELLERY ROLL

Michael was at the National Theatre playing King Ferdinand of Spain in a black doublet and hose covered in jet and black pearls. One afternoon during the run we thought we would nip down the road to the Tower of London to have a look at the English regalia. The Tower is rather like Agatha Christie's play, *The Mousetrap*. It has been open so long that it tends to get ignored by Londoners. It is, in fact, huge value and well worth a visit. It has great romance and colour with its Traitors' Gate, glittering Armoury and all those Beefeaters in their red coats with rosettes on their shoes. The crowning glory is the Jewel House which is darkened for drama, but the gems are alive and aglow. The Queen's Imperial State Crown is worn for coronations and the State Opening of Parliament, and is the biggest and best. It has the ruby which was given by Pedro the Cruel of Castile to Edward, the Black Prince. He wore it in his breastplate, and it was later set in Henry V's helmet for Agincourt and in Richard III's for the Battle of Bosworth Field. It has the sapphire from Edward the Confessor's ring set in the Maltese Cross at the top and Elizabeth I's pearl earrings, snitched from Mary Queen of Scots when her head was cut off. The crown also contains the Second Star of Africa, which is the second largest diamond in the world, and the arches are decorated with a pattern of oak leaves and acorns in memory of that famous tree which sheltered King Charles II.

The stones catch the light in a million different ways, so try to gather lots of shades and pile them on. The colours are not understated. The basis is four diamond colours, plus red (for rubies), green (for emeralds) and blue (for sapphires).

Left: Queen Victoria in 1837 wearing the Imperial State Crown.
Above: Queen Elizabeth II at her coronation in 1953, wearing the same crown. Photograph by Beaton.
Facing page: The Jewellery Roll.

Materials

12-holes-to-inch double-thread
canvas, measuring 12 x 14 inches
(30 x 35 cm)
Beading needle
Size 18 tapestry needle
Sewing needle
Beads and yarns (see below)
Polyester sewing cotton
Jewellery roll

To work

Start by stitching the two rows of pearls edging the 'circlet' of the crown. Then bead all the diamond filigree work: inside the circlet; surrounding the Black Prince Ruby; along the arches; the fleurs-de-lis; the globe; and the Maltese Cross at the top. Then stitch on the coloured stones and the huge Second Star of Africa diamond under the ruby. When doing this, don't follow the grid provided by your canvas. Just pile on as many beads as you can so that the 'stones' are raised and truly encrusted. Sew on the big pearl rounds and drops. I topped some of these with gold filigree cups which are sold in craft shops as jewellery findings. Use cross stitch for the purple and maroon backgrounds. The 'ermine' is stitched in turkeywork (see page 107).

To make up

Stretch your finished canvas. Mine measured 10 x 8 inches (25 x 20 cm), which covers most standard jewellery rolls. Turn under the edge of the canvas and hand-stitch it on to your jewellery roll. Alternatively, line your work and stitch on a series of small pockets made from scraps of the lining.

The crown being transported in stately splendour to a State Opening of Parliament.

Yarns · No. of skeins

	DMC 552 coton perlé no 3	1
	DMC 550 coton perlé no 5 (used double)	3
	DMC 309 coton perlé no 3	2
I	Angora ivory	1 ounce (25 g)
I	Angora black	5 threads

Beads · No. of beads

O	Clear (size 10)	1 pkt
	Silver (size 10)	1 pkt
	Crystal (size 10)	1 pkt
	Frosted silver (size 10)	1 pkt
⌀	Clear bugle (size 2)	1 pkt
●	Clear (size 7)	1 pkt
✦	Clear (size 5)	1 pkt
◇	Crystal glass (¼ inch/6 mm)	1 pkt
◎	Crystal flat cut (⅙ inch/4 mm)	1 pkt
◯	Crystal flat cut (¼ inch/ 6 mm)	1 pkt

'Sweepings'

I used amber, brown, purple, kingfisher and royal blue from one packet.

For the stones

Choose as wide a selection of sizes, shades and shapes as you can muster in ruby, diamond, sapphire and emerald. Include some ⅙ inch (4 mm) beads.

Pearls · No. of beads

	Ivory size ⅙ inch (4 mm) (round)	160
◯	Ivory size ¼ inch (6 mm) (round)	9
⬭	Ivory size 3 (drop)	2
⬭	Ivory size 1 (drop)	6

ALICE BAND

Alice Liddell's constant plea to her friend, Charles Dodgson (better known as Lewis Carroll) was 'Let's PRETEND', and they did. They had a grand time in Oxford. They enjoyed the royal celebrations in the street, the rabbits in Christchurch Meadow, the painting of the dodo in the museum and the gryphons on the fireguard. One July day they rowed up the river and Dodgson continued to weave his tale, which starred Alice, starting from the point where she had just fallen down the rabbit hole. That evening she begged him to write down the story, so he sat up right through the night to do so. Alice received the tale as 'a Christmas present to a dear child in memory of a summer's day.'

But as little girls do, Alice grew up.

Dodgson speaks to her as the White Knight: '"You've only a few yards to go, down the hill and over that little brook, and then you'll be a Queen. But you'll stay and see me off first," he added as Alice turned away with an eager look. "I shan't be long. You'll wait and wave your handkerchief when I get to that turn in the road? I think it'll encourage me, you see".'

Actors, of course, never grow up. That game of 'Let's PRETEND' is how we earn our living. I'm not sure the Cheshire Cat isn't laughing at us.

Bead this simple headband as a Christmas present for a young friend, or make one for yourself in straight black or crystal or red. You could pretend it was made from Whitby jet, or diamonds, or Black Prince rubies.

Below left: The Rev. Charles Dodgson, better known as Lewis Carroll. *Below:* The real Alice in Wonderland, Alice Liddell. *Facing page:* My niece, Daisy, wearing her Cheshire Cat Alice Band.

Materials

12-holes-to inch double-thread
   lightweight canvas, measuring
   5 x 20 inches (12.5 x 50 cm)
Beading needle
Sewing needle
Polyester sewing cotton
Beads (see below)
Padded headband, 1 inch
   (2.5 cm) wide

To work

Following the chart, bead the cat's
eyes, nose and smile first. Once these
are in place, it will be easy to complete
the work.

To make up

Stretch your finished canvas. Turn
under the edges of the canvas and
hand-sew it on to the headband.

Beads	No. of beads
Cream pearl (size 9)	1 pkt
Pink pearl (size 9)	1
Black (size 9)	1 pkt
Black (size 7)	2
Black bugles (size 1, size 2, size 3)	1 pkt of each
Cream pearl bugles (size 1, size 2)	1 pkt of each
Grey pearl (size 10)	1 pkt
Cream oat pearl (size 1)	4
Jonquil crystal glass (⅙ inch/4 mm)	6
Amber (size 7)	1 pkt
Amber bugle (size 1)	1 pkt
Yellow bugle (size 1)	1 pkt
Primrose pearl (size 10)	1 pkt
Amber silver-lined (size 10)	1 pkt
Royal blue (size 11)	1 pkt

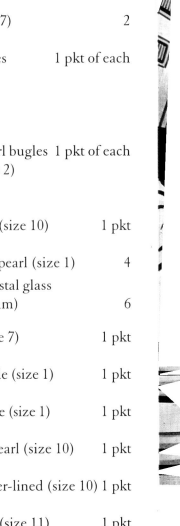

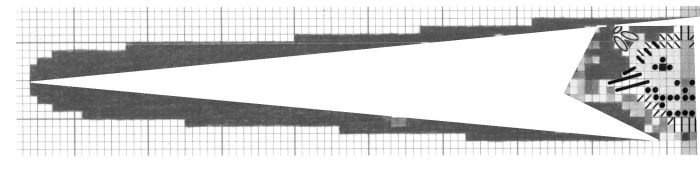

Above: A detail from the Lewis Carroll memorial window in All Saints Church, Daresbury, Cheshire. Dodgson's father was vicar here. The Alice in Wonderland window was created by Geoffrey Webb in 1934.

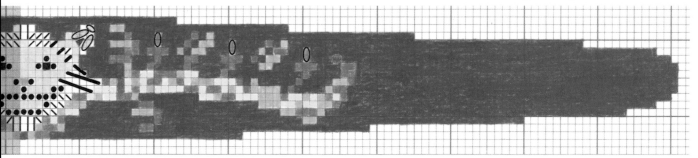

LEOPARD DOORSTOP

Vita Sackville-West wrote a biography of Aphra Behn, the first professional woman playwright. I was performing seven parts in Aphra's *Lucky Chance*, with thirty-two lightning costume changes and all the funny voices and cartoon walks that I could muster. During the day I kept my feet firmly up and read of Aphra and then of Vita and then of Knole, Vita's adored family home 'where the garden has been a garden for four hundred years'. She wrote of its history with such flair and glamour that I decided to point the car Kent-wards as soon as the curtain fell for the final time and I had hung up my seven pairs of boots.

We chose a beautiful day and picnicked in the park among the deer and trees. Knole is a huge grey house with, legend has it, seven courtyards, fifty-two staircases and three hundred and sixty-five rooms. Inside it is aglow with bedhangings of gold tissue and flamingo silk, furniture made of silver beaten over carved wood, Knole sofas and, of course, that leopard. He holds the Sackville arms, is rampant, and cavorts everywhere: above oriel windows, topping pilasters, heading overmantels and supporting furniture. He looks very lively dancing as a doorstop in the Great Hall and very contented sitting like patience on a monument on the newel posts in the Great Stairway.

I decided the carved posts would be the model for my very own Sackville leopard. He would have to be three-dimensional to retain his chutzpah, so I sat down with three pieces of canvas and a pot of faceted jet beads which look satisfyingly spotty. The eyes and mouth are beaded for focus and, at the last minute, I gave him spangled claws at both finger and toe level. I have grown very fond of him presiding over our hall in Shepherd's Bush and now wonder what Vita was thinking of when she decided on leopardskin furs for her going-away outfit.

Left: Knole standing in its deer park. *Above:* Vita, photographed in 1934. *Facing page:* My leopard doorstop dancing with a cavorting Sackville leopard in the Great Hall at Knole.

Materials

10-holes-to inch double-thread
  canvas, 3 pieces measuring
  approximately 14 x 22 inches
  (35 x 55 cm) each
Beads and yarns (see below)
1¼ yards (1 metre) heavyweight
  interfacing
Size 18 tapestry needle
Beading needle
Sewing needle
Polyester sewing cotton
Weighted filling
Green fabric for bottom

To work

Start by working the black outline of
the leopard, then add the pewter beading and fill in the picture according to
the chart. All is worked in tent stitch
except the silky shield, which is worked
in cross stitch, as shown on the chart.

To make up

Stretch your three finished canvases.
With right sides together, stitch the
three sides of the leopard together.
Turn right sides out and oversew the
seams in 443 golden brown and the
coffee brown yarns, where applicable.
Cut out the three leopard shapes from
the interfacing, used double. Tack
each set of interfacing on to the wrong
side of the tapestry. Stuff with your
filling. (I used rice which I had first
sterilized in a warm oven but you
could also use dried beans.) Cut the
green fabric to fit the bottom, plus a
seam allowance. Turn under the seam
allowance all round and stitch to the
bottom of the leopard. Keep your
stitches small or the filling may ooze
out.

Facing page: The Great Hall at Knole.
Left: The Sackville leopard on the newel post
in the Great Staircase. He was my model.

Yarns	*No. of skeins*
Paterna Persian Yarns	
220 black	2
442 golden brown	1
443 golden brown	11
444 golden brown	11
445 golden brown	1
plus DMC ecru coton perlé no 3	6
420 coffee brown	1
421 coffee brown	1
422 coffee brown	2
423 coffee brown	2
424 coffee brown	1
660 pine green	2
661 pine green	2
660 pine green	1 thread
661 pine green	2 threads
423 coffee brown	1 thread
640 khaki	2 threads
424 coffee brown	1 thread
641 khaki	2 threads

Cottons (or equivalent silks):

DMC 666 coton perlé no 3	1
DMC 797 coton perlé no 3	1
DMC 433 coton perlé no 3	1
DMC 4712 rayonne	1
Thick gold metallic yarn 22 yards (20 metres)	

Beads	*No. of beads*
Pewter (¼ inch/6 mm)	100
Pewter (⅓ inch/8 mm)	50
Amber (size 10)	1 pkt
Amber (size 7)	1 pkt
Red (size 10)	1 pkt
Red (size 7)	1 pkt
Black (size 10)	1 pkt
Embroidery stones (small)	12

Note: Paterna yarns are sold as Paternayan in the U.S.

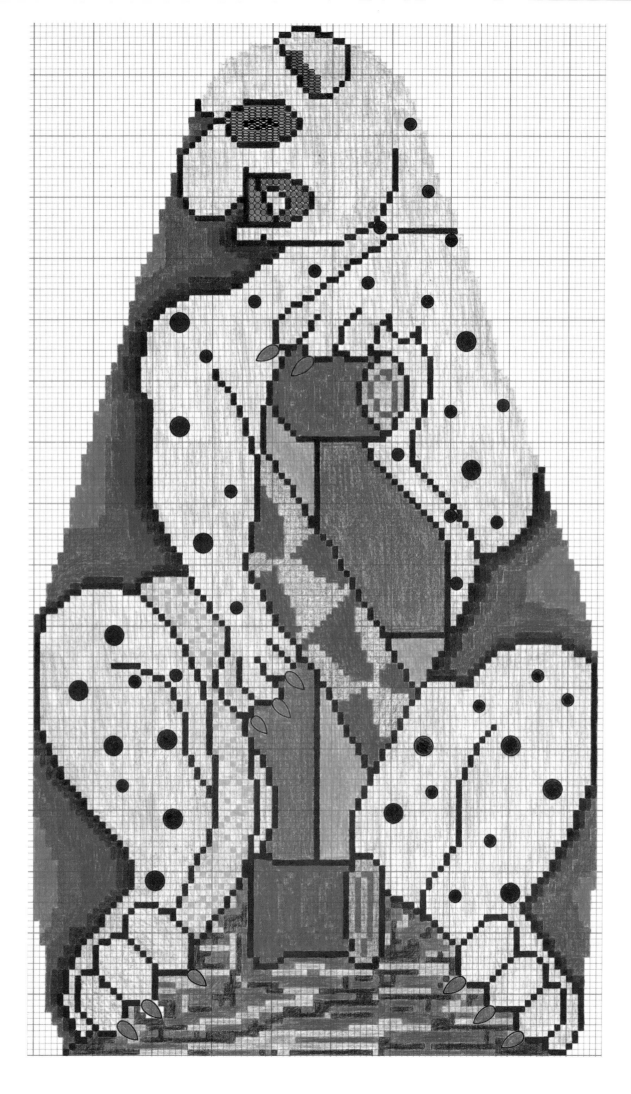

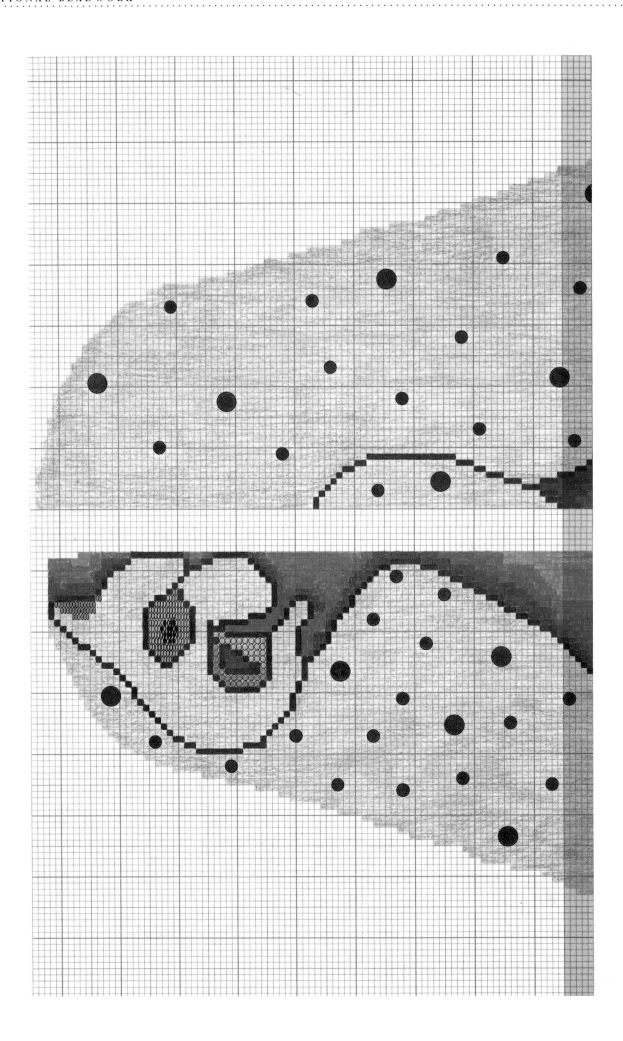

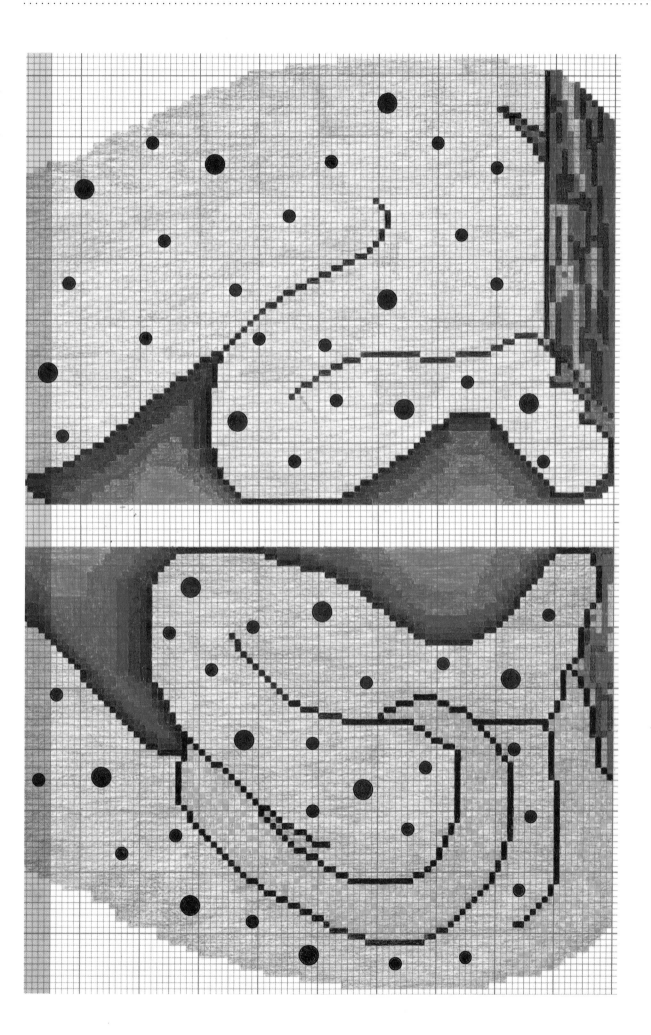

SUNLIGHT SPONGE BAG

Michael had shaved his head and was up at the Liverpool Everyman Theatre doing a show about Chernobyl. One Sunday we took a ferry 'cross the Mersey to soak up a bit of cheer from Port Sunlight. Every British child of my generation has heard of Sunlight soap because the original business brains behind it, William Hesketh Lever, was well aware of the power of advertising. He packaged his top-quality bars and marked them all with his sunshine logo. He also packaged his workforce and built them a beautiful – and the first-ever – garden suburb to live in. This is Port Sunlight and it is a delight. He gave everyone the luxury of a bath-room, individual architecture and a garden. 'A home requires a greensward in front of it as much as a cup requires a saucer.' He even gave the children lit-tle patches of land to grow things on.

His collection of treasures there, housed in the Lady Lever Art Gallery, is as diverse as the houses that sur-round it. He gathered the pieces to cel-ebrate craftsmanship as art, because he believed in art as a power for good, and in memory of his wife.

I beaded the design from a cabinet decorated with rolled paper because it seemed so much like his own trade-mark. Stitch more or less of the back-ground to fit your bag; it is packaging and can be made to fit anything.

Left: The beautiful paperwork cabinet from which I took a detail. *Above:* The side of the cabinet, on its stand, which was made in the 1780s. *Facing page:* My sponge bag.

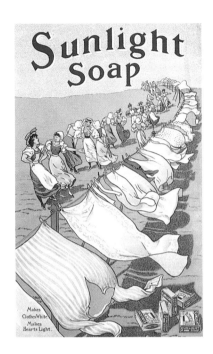

Materials

8-holes-to-inch double-thread canvas,
    measuring approximately
    14 x 28 inches (35 x 70 cm)
Beads and yarns (see below)
Size 18 tapestry needle
Beading needle
Sewing needle
Polyester sewing cotton
Folding sponge bag for toiletries,
    cosmetics, etc
Black bias binding

To work

Start by beading the pale blue centre of
the sunburst and build up from there.
Stitch on the pearl swag and lay on the
gold 'tassels' with a couching stitch
(see page 108). Use the thin gold
metallic yarn to secure the laid threads
of thick gold metallic yarn. Stitch on
the bead edging in a position to fit your
bag. Complete the backgrounds in
cross stitch. When stitching the beige
background, use the DMC 739 coton
perlé no 3 to stitch the understroke of
the cross stitch and DMC 951 coton
perlé no 3 for the top stroke.

To make up

Stretch your finished canvas. Machine-
stitch a black bias binding strip all
round your bag. Turn under the edges
of your canvas and hand-stitch on to
the bias binding. When the bag gets a
bit steamy and dog-eared, it will be
easy to unstitch the canvas and put it
on a new bag.

Some examples of Lord Leverhulme's
advertising campaign for his famous
Sunlight soap.

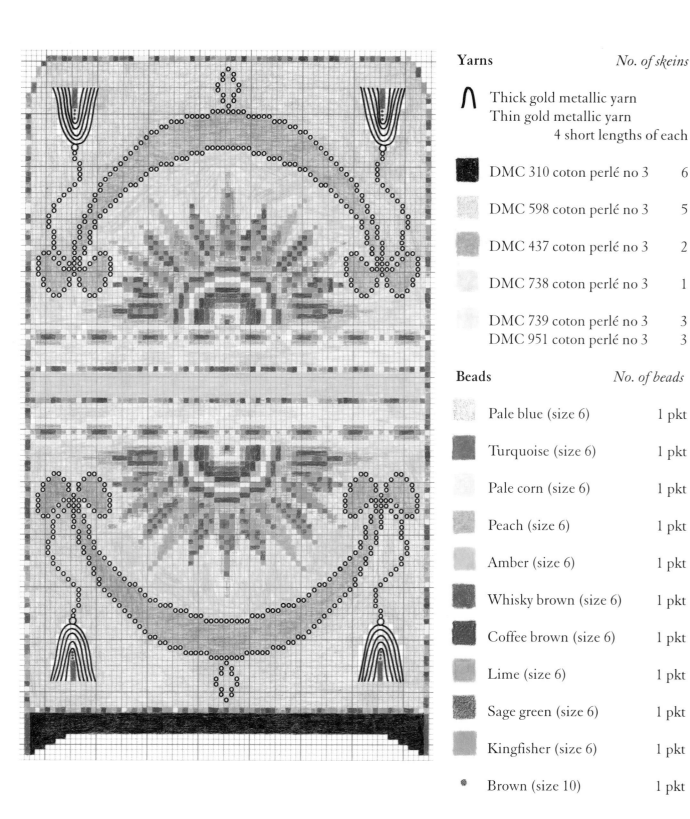

Yarns *No. of skeins*

∩ Thick gold metallic yarn
 Thin gold metallic yarn
  4 short lengths of each

DMC 310 coton perlé no 3   6

DMC 598 coton perlé no 3   5

DMC 437 coton perlé no 3   2

DMC 738 coton perlé no 3   1

DMC 739 coton perlé no 3   3
DMC 951 coton perlé no 3   3

Beads *No. of beads*

Pale blue (size 6)   1 pkt

Turquoise (size 6)   1 pkt

Pale corn (size 6)   1 pkt

Peach (size 6)   1 pkt

Amber (size 6)   1 pkt

Whisky brown (size 6)   1 pkt

Coffee brown (size 6)   1 pkt

Lime (size 6)   1 pkt

Sage green (size 6)   1 pkt

Kingfisher (size 6)   1 pkt

• Brown (size 10)   1 pkt

Pearls

o A mixture of pale pink and ivory,
 sizes ¹⁄₁₂ inch (2 mm) and ⅙ inch
 (4 mm). Use 300 pearls.

69

DRUM PINCUSHION

Marlene Dietrich had beads sewn on to her gowns in vertical rows. This way they shimmered more but weighed less than solid beadwork. Ellen Terry was cleverer. She had real beetles' wings, which are as light as gossamer, sewn on to her Lady Macbeth frock. W. Graham Robertson described her: 'Long plaits of deep red hair fell from under a purple veil over a robe of green upon which iridescent wings of beetles glittered like emeralds and a great wine coloured cloak, gold embroidered, swept from her shoulders. The effect was barbaric.'

We saw her costume at Smallhythe, Ellen's country cottage in Kent, which is packed with interest. I had seen the brilliant show by Tina Gray, my pal and fellow stitcher, about *Our Ellen*, so I already felt I knew her. She was a good egg. When her actor-manager, Henry Irving, received his knighthood, the company and crew christened her 'Lady Darling' to match. In the painting by Watts she is famously *Choosing* between the sweet-smelling but humble violet and the grand camellia, which has no perfume. Apparently, she herself thought this conceit too dull for words and was determined to juggle everything: being a wife, a mother and a *bonne viveuse*. Not a bad example to set.

Left: A souvenir programme of the Irving/Terry production of *Macbeth*. *Above:* The famous Sargent portrait of Ellen Terry as Lady Macbeth. *Facing page:* 'A drum, a drum, Macbeth doth come.' My pincushion, photographed with the outrageous head-dress of a crown and magenta plaits, at Smallhythe in Kent.

Materials

10-holes-to-inch double-thread
 canvas, 2 pieces each measuring
 8 inches square
 (20 cm square)
16-holes-to-inch single-thread canvas,
 measuring 18 x 6½ inches
 (45 x 16.25 cm)
Beading needle
Size 18 tapestry needle
Sewing needle
Beads and yarns (see below)
Polyester sewing cotton
2¾ yards (2.5 metres) fine cord
Polyester lining, 2 pieces each
 measuring 8 inches square
 (20 cm square) and
 1 piece measuring 18 x 6½ inches
 (45 x 16.25 cm)
Steel wool for filling

To work

Working from the chart, outline the shape of the beetles' wings in back stitch with a fine gold metallic thread. Fill these in with your collection of beads. Pile on as many as possible, ignoring the exact spacing of your canvas, to create encrusted, raised shapes. Work the background in cross stitch. Work the base in cross stitch too. The side panel is a simple bargello pattern which is easy to follow from the chart. The stitches are straight and are each worked over two threads of canvas. You need to stitch 100 rows.

To make up

Stretch your three pieces of finished work. Using these as a pattern and leaving a ½-inch (12-mm) seam allowance, cut out three pieces of lining. Machine-stitch the top and bottom lining pieces to the long side strip and fill with the steel wool. Stitch up the side seam. With right sides together, stitch the side tapestry around the beetle-winged top. Join the side seam on the outside with another row of bargello stitching and then slip in your pincushion. Stitch on the bottom piece. Finish the work by sewing a fine cord round the top and bottom edges.

Above: George Frederick Watts' portrait of Ellen Terry *Choosing.*

Left: A close-up of the beetles' wings used to decorate Ellen's dress.

Side

Top

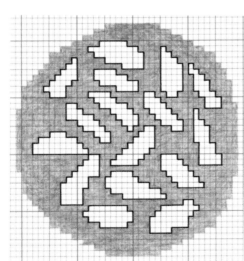

Bottom

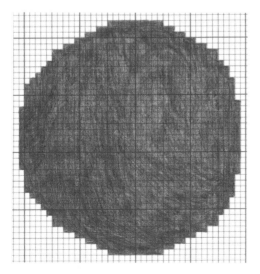

Yarns	*No. of skeins*
DMC 504 coton perlé no 3	3
DMC 937 coton perlé no 3	3
DMC 321 coton perlé no 3	1
DMC 902 coton perlé no 3	1
DMC 900 coton perlé no 3	1
DMC 352 coton perlé no 3	1
⌐ Fine bronze metallic thread	
8¾ yards (8 metres)	

Beads

Choose as many different green beads as you can find. You need only a few of each. Alternatively, you could choose a couple of packets of mixed greens. I used:

	Bottle green (size 7)	1 pkt
	Emerald green (size 7)	1 pkt
	Bottle green (size 10)	1 pkt
	Emerald green (size 10)	1 pkt
	Lime green (size 10)	1 pkt
	Green/bronze mix (size 10)	1 pkt
	Deep green metallic (size 10)	1 pkt

73

OSCAR'S HANDBAG

As the vagaries of life will have it, on 25 May 1895 it was announced that the famous actor-manager, Henry Irving, was to be the first theatrical knight, bringing honour to the whole, hitherto disreputable, profession; and on that same day the playwright Oscar Wilde was sentenced to two years' hard labour. During his trial, the wicked caricature shown here was used in evidence against him, much to the horror of its executor, Max Beerbohm. Max wrote some reference notes for it: 'Luxury – hair curled…huge rings – fat white hands – pointed fingers – Louis Quinze – cane vast malmaison –

catlike tread – heavy shoulders – enormous dowager – or schoolboy… Effeminate, but vitality of twenty men. Magnetism – authority.'

You can see the drawing in the Ashmolean Museum, Oxford. I looked it up when I was touring in *The Importance of Being Earnest*. I have used my beads sparingly here to capture the essence of Beerbohm's drawing: the opulence of Oscar's jewellery, his dapper cane, his taut waistcoat just about held together by the pearl buttons. Like Miss Prism, I use my bag with joy and very much in evidence for the importance of being Oscar.

Facing page: Oscar's Handbag photographed front of house at the Aldwych Theatre, London. *Right:* Oscar in New York in 1882.

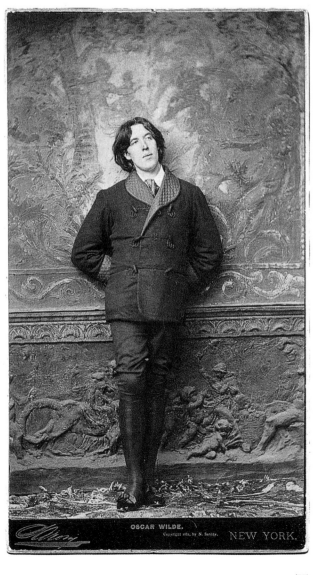

OSCAR WILDE.
Copyright 1882, by N. Sarony.
NEW YORK.

Above: Max on Max –
a self-portrait.
Facing page: Michael
Redgrave as Jack and
Margaret Rutherford as
Miss Prism. 'The bag is
undoubtedly mine. I am
delighted to have it so
unexpectedly restored to
me. It has been a *great*
inconvenience being
without it all these years.
Right: The Beerbohm
caricature of Oscar.

Above: The design for my
Gwendolen costume in
Acts 2 and 3, designed by
Sarah-Jane McClelland.

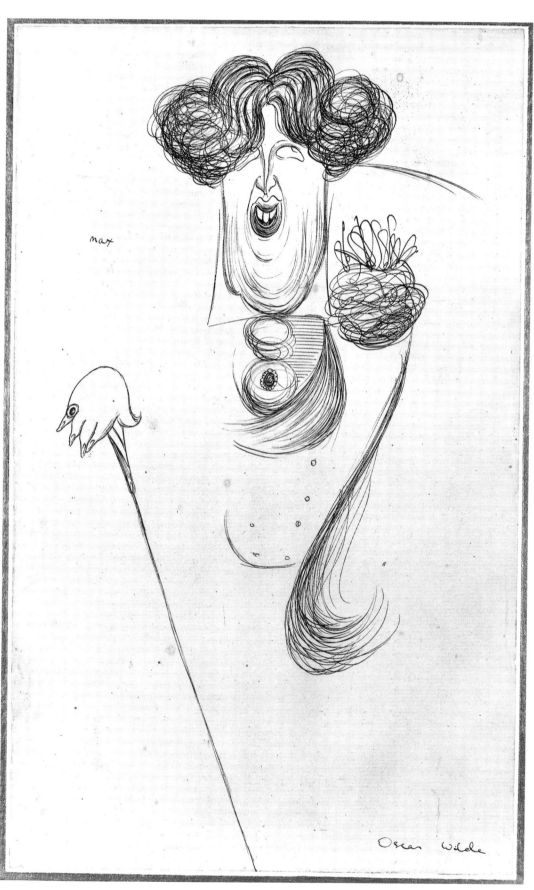

Materials

10-holes-to-inch double-thread
    canvas (to fit your chosen bag
    clasp)
Size 18 tapestry needle
Beading needle
Sewing needle
Beads and yarns (see below)
Polyester sewing cotton
Bag clasp
Lining fabric

To work

Start by working the black outline of
the figure, then fill in the picture
according to the chart. It is all worked
in tent stitch, using one thread, except
for the following:

• The tie knot is a smooth spider's web
(see page 108).

• The hair and carnation petals are
bullion knots (see page 108). The
foundation spokes for both of these are
marked on the chart.

• The border of the design is worked
with two threads of DMC coton perlé
no 3 in long stitch over two threads of
canvas.

• The cane is worked with two threads
of DMC coton perlé no 3 forming a
cross stitch over the background.

The black background beyond the border of the design is stitched to a size
suitable for your clasp.

To make up

Stretch your finished canvas. Make up
according to the measurements of your
chosen bag clasp. You can make a simple tote bag shape or, by adding gus-
sets, you can create a fuller carpet bag
shape reminiscent of Oscar's play.

Yarns	*No. of skeins*
DMC noir tapestry wool	1
DMC blanc	1
DMC ecru	1
DMC 7191	1
DMC 7624	2
DMC 7622	2
DMC 7618	1

Cottons	*No. of skeins*
DMC 890 coton perlé no 3	1
DMC 700 coton perlé no 3	1
DMC 955 coton perlé no 3	1
DMC 943 coton perlé no 3	1
DMC 310 coton perlé no 3	4
Black/silver metallic yarn	1
DMC 504 coton perlé no 3	5

Beads	*No. of beads*
Pearl (⅙ inch/4 mm)	12
Black metallic (size 10)	1 pkt
Emerald (size 10)	1 pkt
Gold metallic (size 10)	1 pkt

Note: The bag itself is
constructed around the
clasp of the bag, so buy
a clasp that you like and
then plan the shape and
size of the bag
accordingly.

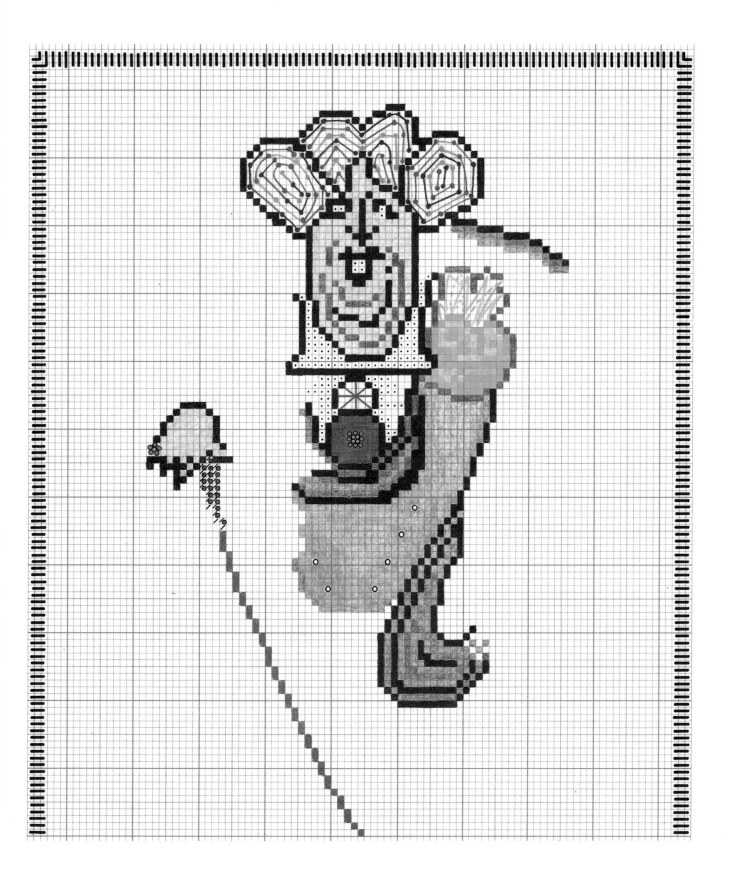

COMFORT PILLOW

Louis Comfort Tiffany once wrote 'It is curious, is it not, that line and form disappear at a short distance, while colour remains visible much longer? It is fairly certain – isn't it? – that the eyes of children at first see only coloured surfaces…colour and movement, not form, are our earliest impressions.' His favourite colour was yellow. He was the eccentric son of Charles, the jeweller, at whose store Holly Golightly had her breakfast; and he was brought up surrounded by luxury and opulence. Through much experiment he discovered how to make coloured glass without painting it. He added various metallic oxides to the traditional composition. His yellow came from uranium, red from gold, green from iron oxide and blue from cobalt oxide. He thought that coloured glass windows were a good wheeze for urban dwellings where the outlooks would otherwise be dingy and confined and, indeed, this panel has brought exotic cheer to our bedroom.

For my bash at painting with glass I have used many, many different shades of beads. At least I didn't have to blow them first! The lead divisions give you a good structure. Choose a dominant colour for each panel of background, but let many other shades bleed in from neighbouring panels. You can't go wrong. You can only create waves of beautiful colour.

Below: Louis Comfort Tiffany. *Bottom:* The glassworks at the Tiffany Studios. *Facing page:* My pillow.

Materials

12-holes-to-inch double-thread
    canvas, measuring approximately
    12 x 15 inches
    (30 x 37.5 cm)
Beads and yarns (see below)
Size 18 tapestry needle
Beading needle
Sewing needle
Polyester sewing cotton
Enough dry lavender to fill the
    cushion
2 pieces of thick cotton, each
    measuring approximately
    12 x 15 inches (30 x 37.5 cm)
Backing fabric, measuring
    approximately 12 x 15 inches
    (30 x 37.5 cm)
1½ yards (1.25 metres) edging cord

To work

Following the chart, stitch in the
framework provided by the charcoal
stitching. Then bead the branches, parrot, flowers and leaves. Finally, bead
each panel of background separately.

To make up

Stretch your finished canvas. Use it as a
pattern to cut out the backing fabric,
plus a ½-inch (12-mm) seam allowance.
With right sides together, stitch on
three sides of your backing silk to the
canvas. Turn right sides out. Make a
cushion pad from the piece of featherproof fabric (see page 106) and fill with
the dry lavender. Pop this pad inside
the canvas cushion. Stitch up the
fourth seam. Edge the cushion with
the cord.

The panel of leaded Favrile glass, produced by
the Tiffany Studios in New York c. 1900-1910.

Yarn *No. of skeins*

❜ DMC 413 coton perlé no 3   2

Beads

Choose beads in sizes 9-11, but don't feel you have to stick to one size only as different sizes give different shadings of colour. Just make sure you don't choose any beads that are too big.

For the branches

 2 browns (glass metallic)
1 pkt of each

For the head

 2 oranges (silver-lined, cut)
1 pkt of each
 2 ambers (lustre, metallic)
1 pkt of each
 Peach pearl (for the beak) 1 bead

 Black (size 8) (for the eye) 1 bead

For the body

 10 greens (lime, emerald, bottle green, lustre, light pearl, mid pearl, metallic, matt olive, matt bottle green, gun metal)
1 pkt of each

 2 blues (metallic, glass)
1 pkt of each
 1 purple (glass)   1 pkt

The shading on the parrot and magnolias is for guidance only. Fill in each panel of shading using whichever shade of beads you wish.

For the white clematis

3 whites (pearl white, matt white, blush)   1 pkt of each

For the pink magnolias

8 pinks (metallic, garnet, claret, rose cut, pink lustre, pink pearl, pale pink pearl, pink crystal)   1 pkt of each

2 blues (blue pearl, blue crystal)   1 pkt of each
1 purple   1 pkt

For the leaves

2 turquoises (cut, pearl)   1 pkt of each
4 greens (lime, emerald, bottle green, lustre)   1 pkt of each

Background

2 mauves (pearl, lustre)   1 pkt of each
1 deep peach (lustre)   1 pkt

Metallics (mixed)   1 pkt

6 yellows (opaque, lemon, graded, primrose, cut, pearl)   1 pkt of each
8 blues (turquoise pearl and lustre, metallic, royal purple, matt, mercury, turquoise [size 9], turquoise graded [size 9])   1 pkt of each

BYRON'S SLIM VOLUME

Newstead Abbey is an easy drive from Nottingham Play-house where I was opening in Alan Ayckbourn's *Bedroom Farce*, not for the first or the last time. Lord Byron inherited the Old Priory when he was ten years old and, when he took possession at twenty-one, it was the beginning of his bedroom farce. 'I have to walk half a mile to my bedchamber,' he wrote, as the only habitable living quarters were at the opposite end of the building. He restored his bedroom bit by bit as he could afford it, bringing in a splendid four-poster bed, rich bed hangings, carpets and wallpaper. The only snag was that he forgot to mend the roof first, so it was all a bit short-lived. He settled for using the Great Hall as his range for pistol practise, and decided to block off a passage in the East Cloister and treat himself to a plunge bath. He wisely

hung on to the tin bath in his bedroom, though, for those mornings when he couldn't face that chilly dash down to the crypt. Next to his bedroom is the Prior's Oratory, which was haunted by the Black Friar. Byron used to hear him wandering about of an evening and wrote of this in *Don Juan*. In 1817 Byron sold Newstead to his best friend for £94,000.

I have stitched Don Juan's Firebird into a book cover, having seen a fabulous Italian table inlaid with semi-precious stones at Newstead. You don't have to use exactly the same shades that I have chosen; just be sure to bead your work in 'patches' to reflect the bird's plumage and the mosaic stones. Try to track down old beads for this, or break down some new ones. The background area is easy to alter to fit the shape of your book.

Facing page: The beaded bookcover. *Right:* One of the most famous portraits of Byron, painted by Thomas Phillips in 1813.

Materials
12-holes-to-inch double-thread
   antique brown canvas, measuring
   approximately 13 x 16 inches
   (32.5 x 40 cm) or so (but don't for-
   get to measure your book first!)
Beads and yarns (see below)
Size 18 tapestry needle
Beading needle
Sewing needle
Polyester sewing cotton
Backing silk, measuring
   approximately 13 x 20 inches
   (32.5 x 50 cm), according
   to the size of your book
Cord and tassel bookmark

To work
Start by beading the beak and work
from the chart across and downwards.
The white bugle beads on the wings
are stitched flush to each other, disre-
garding the grid of the canvas. When
the bird is completed, stitch the flame
outline in a position to fit the book you
wish to cover. Be sure to measure your
book when it is closed. Stitch in the
background with tent stitch. This covers the canvas scantily but contributes
to the antique look.

To make up
Stretch your finished canvas. Turn
under the edges of the canvas and
hand-stitch it to your backing silk.
Hand-stitch flaps of the backing fabric
to the left- and right-hand sides of the
backed canvas. The width of each flap
should be at least 2 inches (5 cm).
Attach the cord and tassel bookmark,
insert the book and slip in the bookmark.

Left: Detail of the Italianate table top at Newstead Abbey, with my firebird bottom right. *Above:* The table in situ in Newstead Abbey.

89

Yarns   *No. of skeins*

DMC 606 coton perlé no 3   1

DMC 838 coton perlé no 3   2

DMC 800 coton perlé no 3   1

DMC 799 coton perlé no 3   1

DMC 310 coton perlé no 3   4

Beads

Whites   *No. of beads*

Milk opaque (size 10)   1 pkt

White opaque (size 10)   1 pkt

Silver frosted (size 10)   1 pkt

Cream pearl (size 10)   1 pkt

White cut (size 3)   1 pkt

Pink (size 10)   1 pkt

Flames

Orange silver-lined (size 11) 1 pkt

Orange cut (size 3)   1 pkt

Red cut (size 3)   1 pkt

Orange (size 10)   1 pkt

Red (size 10)   1 pkt

Red rainbow (size 9)   1 pkt

Ambers

Amber silver-lined (size 11) 1 pkt

Amber cut (size 3)   1 pkt

Browns

Brown (size 10)   1 pkt

Metallic mixture cut (size 3) 1 pkt

Brown crystal (size 10)   1 pkt

Blacks

Black (size 10)   1 pkt

Black cut (size 3)   1 pkt

Bugles

Cream (size 1)   1 pkt

White (size 2)   1 pkt

Black (size 1)   1 pkt

FLYING FISH COASTER

Los Angeles is art deco. Art deco epitomizes all that was glamour and escapism in Hollywood's heyday: Busby Berkeley movies, the mask-like elegance of the hallowed golden Oscar itself. It soon became something that everyone could share, as mass production brought deco design into every five-and-dime store. There is a lot of

Facing page: The Flying Fish Coaster. *Right:* A statue of the Oscar award. *Below:* The outrageous deco Bruin Theater in Westwood Village, Los Angeles.

new building in Los Angeles now, but the skyline on Sunset at sunset is still pure magic.

Michael and I were staying on the Boulevard and drove right along it until we met the Pacific Ocean. Samson, our son, was four months old and this was his first view of the sea. He sat under his huge white sun-hat gossiping to the seagulls while we had a wonderful lunch at Gladstones, the best fish restaurant ever. I thought I would stitch something to remember it by.

I have used a bigger mesh of canvas than usual, which means you can cover ground quicker if you plan to make two or twelve coasters. Change the red and yellow colours, if you fancy, to suit your colour scheme. The white wave and the black fish will keep the deco feel. The mixture of shades, though, is important for an easy but rich background. The small black edging beads are used discreetly on the same principle as for the Tile Chair Seat (see pages 8-11).

Materials

10-holes-to-inch double-thread
  canvas, measuring approximately
  14 inches square
  (35 cm square)
Beading needle
Sewing needle
Beads (see below)
Polyester sewing cotton
Non-slip backing fabric, measuring
  approximately 14 inches square
  (35 cm square)

To work

Start by using your black beads to outline the shape of the fish, the wave and
the border. Complete the detail in the
fish and wave and the rest will be plain
sailing. Mix the red beads in a bowl so
you can stitch them at random.

To make up

Stretch your finished canvas. With
right sides together, stitch on the backing fabric, leaving a 4-inch (10-cm)
gap. Turn right sides out, sew up the
gap and stitch on the edging beads.

Above: The White Cap Plate
on which I based my design.
Left: The Brown Derby
restaurant on Wilshire
Boulevard in Los Angeles.

Beads   *No. of beads*

	Black (size 8)	2 pkts
	Green opaque (size 8)	1 pkt
	Green lustre (size 8)	1 pkt
	Green pearl (size 8)	1 pkt
	Frosted white cut (size 2)	1 pkt
•	White opaque (size 8)	1 pkt
	White pearl (size 8)	1 pkt

	Brown lustre (size 8)	1 pkt
	Brown matt (size 10)	1 pkt
	Purple metallic (size 8)	1 pkt
	Reds: mixture of 3 shades (size 8)	5 pkts in total
	Yellow opaque (size 8)	2 pkts
	Edging beads: black opaque (size 6)	1 pkt

CLOWN TOY BAG

Clowns, court jesters, fools, harlequins and pierrots have been standing up on their two feet and raising a laugh or a tear since the beginning of time. I thought it would be fun to try to pass on some of the happiness they have brought to our baby, Samson.

We found the scatty-haired lad in this poster on a visit to the wondrous Bethnal Green Museum of Childhood in the East End of London. It is an image from an old game board which was, in fact, intended for adults. The game was not competitive; the object was for everyone to meet in the centre of the board at the same time and the players would lay bets during the course of the game.

I have used rug canvas as I wanted to make a toy bag big enough to be of real use and so the clown would be bold and jolly. Use any bright beads you have or like; this is the project for any broken strings already in your bead box. Size is immaterial as there is no need to keep to the grid of the canvas. You need long thin beads for the collar and cuffs – size 3 bugles would be fine. I used these long diamond ones which came from a jazzy necklace donated by Samson's glamorous great-godmother, Rita. The greater the variety of beads you gather, the more extraordinary and fascinating the clown will be to its owner.

Materials

6-holes-to-inch rug canvas, 2 pieces
    each measuring approximately
    20 x 23 inches (50 x 57.5 cm) and
    2 pieces each measuring approxi-
    mately 14 x 23 inches
    (35 x 57.5 cm)
Beads and yarns (see below)
Size 18 tapestry needle
Beading needle
Sewing needle

Polyester sewing cotton
Plastic canvas for stiffening, 2 pieces
    each measuring approximately
    20 x 23 inches (50 x 57.5 cm) and
    2 pieces each measuring
    approximately 14 x 23 inches
    (35 x 57.5 cm)
Lining fabric, 2 pieces each measuring
    approximately 20 x 23 inches
    (50 x 57.5 cm) and 2 pieces each
    measuring approximately
    14 x 23 inches (35 x 57.5 cm)
Sturdy fabric for bottom, 1 piece
    measuring approximately
    20 x 14 inches (50 x 35 cm)
Cord for handles

Below: The original game board. *Facing page:* Our son Samson with his toy bag in his bedroom at home.

To work

Start by cross stitching the black out-lines of the clown's costume. Bead each panel with a handful of bright beads as you collect them. Size ⅕ inch (5 mm) fits evenly on the canvas, but I mainly went for the bolder ¼ inch (6 mm) and disregarded the canvas grid. The feet, face, hands and treasure sack are cross-stitched. Embroider the features on top of the face as shown on the chart. Either cross stitch your initials, or use bullion knots (see page 108) to match the hair. The juggling club is sewn with cross stitch, which is then oversewn with random long stitch for texture. Mark out the back panel of the bag so it is the same size as the front. I made each side only sixty stitches wide. Sprinkle about five stars on each side panel and about eight on the back. Complete all backgrounds with navy blue cross stitch.

To make up

Stretch your four finished canvases and trim them, leaving a ½-inch (12-mm) seam allowance all the way round. Bind the side seams together with navy blue tapestry yarn. Hand-sew the sturdy fabric for the bottom in place. Tack four pieces of plastic canvas to the inside for stiffening, turn in the top all the way round and line the sides and bottom with the lining fabric. Make two handles from the cord and stitch them securely in position.

All coton perlés are used double:

Yarns	No. of skeins
DMC 310 coton perlé no 3	3
DMC blanc neige coton perlé no 3	1
DMC 972 coton perlé no 3	6
DMC 828 coton perlé no 3	2
DMC 321 coton perlé no 3	1
DMC 7782 tapestry yarn	1
DMC 7781 tapestry yarn	1
DMC 7783 tapestry yarn	1
Paterna yarn mustard 711	1
Paterna yarn navy blue 570	4 hanks

Beads	No. of beads
Diamond-shaped or silver bugle (size 3) for collar and cuffs	about 16
Amber (⁴⁄₁₀ inch/10 mm) for pompons	2
Pearls (²⁄₁₀ inch/5 mm) for buttons	5
For the suit, you will need at least 500 beads, depending on the size used.	

Above: An early 19th-century engraving showing Harlequin and Pantaloon in pantomine.

Note: Paterna yarns are sold as Paternayan in the U.S.

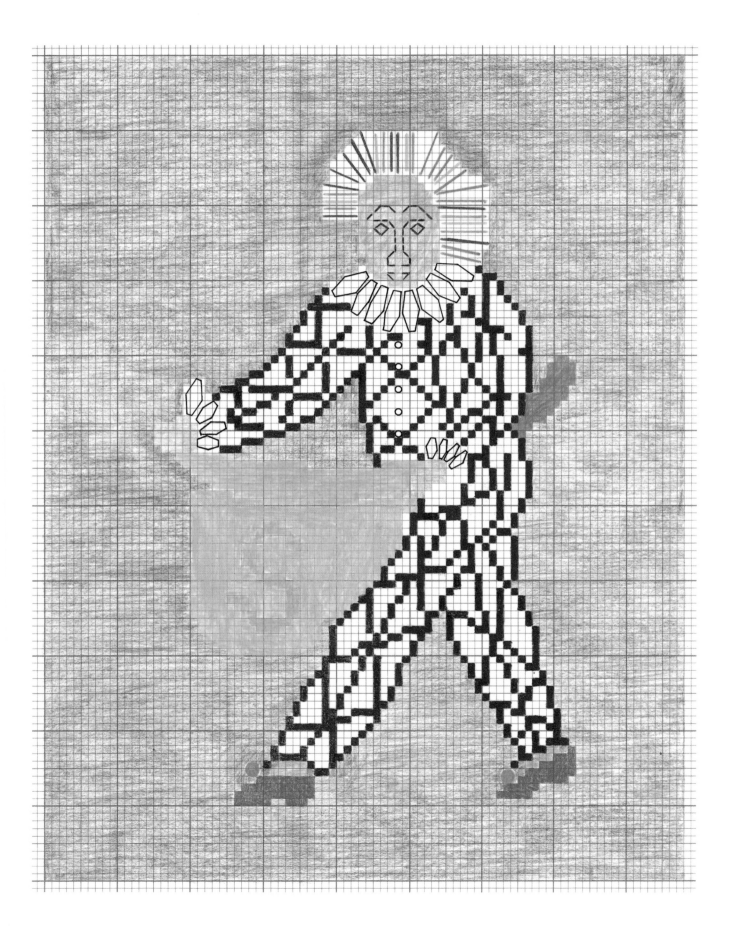

FIRST-NIGHT BAG

I went to New York to see the first night of *Me and My Girl* on Broadway and my best friend, Lisa Zeff. I didn't stop moving. I tapped down 42nd Street, I chugged round Manhattan on the cityline ferry and I shrieked up and down in those see-through elevators. We had a first-night supper in Sardi's, Bloody Marys for Sunday brunch in SoHo, a Hershey bar on top of the Empire State Building. I completely wore through my espadrilles. It was when I was shooting down to Battery Park on the roaring subway that I began noticing the subway signs. They are lovely. They were designed by Heins and LeFarge to make the stations look jolly and less like the Black Hole of Calcutta. They were a language for immigrants. There are the beavers at Astor Place, the locomotive at Grand

Central and the ship at Columbus Circle. It is a language of colour.

I decided to stitch the tulips of Atlantic Avenue so that I could A to Zee it for my pal, Ms Zeff. Stitch your own initial in the space provided. I have used spring flower colours: tulip yellow on the front, crocus purple on the back with a topping of snowdrop silver. I used lashings of different purples. Just mix all you can lay your hands on in a bowl and stitch quickly, using whichever beads come to hand.

Top: A jam-packed, graffiti-covered, subway train.
Left: A New York sign pointing to two of the most famous streets in the world.
Below: The wonderful subway sign at Atlantic Avenue.
Facing page: The bag I made for Lisa Zeff.

Beads

No. of beads

Five yellows

■	Honey crystal (size 10)	1 pkt
■	Daffodil cut (size 3)	1 pkt
■	Yellow pearl (size 10)	1 pkt
■	Pale yellow pearl (size 10)	1 pkt
■	Peach pearl (size 10)	1 pkt

Three pearls

•	White (size 10)	1 pkt
	Cream (size 10)	1 pkt
■	Lustre (size 10)	1 pkt

Three greens

■	Matt graded (size 10)	1 pkt
	Metallic (size 10)	1 pkt
	Deep bottle green (size 10)	1 pkt

■	Silver cut (size 2)	1 pkt
●	Amber pebble ⅙ inch (4 mm)	4
●	Amber cut glass ⅙ inch (4 mm)	2
■	Mixture of purples: you will need one packet each of three or four different shades. I used a capful each of about twelve different shades, but you don't have to follow suit.	

Materials

12-holes-to-inch double-thread
 canvas, measuring approximately
 12 x 5 inches (30 x 12.5 cm)
Beading needle
Sewing needle
Beads (see below)
Polyester sewing cotton
Silk for lining and sides of bag
Plastic canvas
Cords for handles

To work

Start by beading the mid-yellow square in the middle of the work: rows 17 and 18 up from the bottom of the chart, rows 16 and 17 in from the sides. You now have a frame. Bead inwards from this, using the pearl and yellow beads, beading your initial last. Fill in the background of green beads. Now bead outwards from your original square, completing the key pattern. Bead the silver surround and the top, then carefully count and bead the silver frame to the back. It is identical in size to the front: 101 x 65 beads. Fill in with your purple mixture.

To make up

Stretch your finished canvas and trim it, leaving a ½-inch (12-mm) seam allowance all the way round. Make the basic shape of the clutch bag from the plastic canvas to fit your beadwork.

Cover each piece of plastic canvas with a thin layer of padding and then lining fabric. Do this with fabric glue, if you wish. Join the bag pieces together, attaching cord for the handles to the inside. Cover each cord end with a patch of lining. Hand-sew on the beadwork to form the outside cover.

The measurements shown here are simply a guide – your bag may be bigger or smaller.

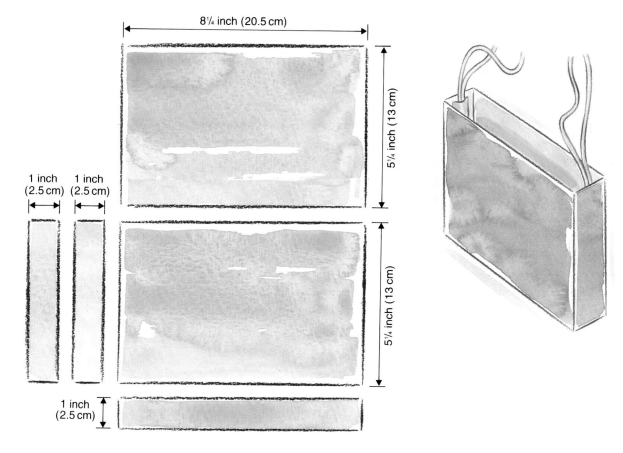

8¼ inch (20.5 cm)

5¼ inch (13 cm)

5¼ inch (13 cm)

1 inch (2.5 cm)   1 inch (2.5 cm)

1 inch (2.5 cm)

BASIC SEWING TECHNIQUES

Beading

This is very easy. Use ordinary tent stitch and thread a bead through your needle every time it comes to the front of the work. Each bead will be secured in place and, once you have the knack, you will soon find you can work quickly. I find it helpful to work on a table, rather than attempt beading on my lap, and I stitch with my dominant hand and thread the bead on with the other.

Equipment

You need very few pieces of equipment for beading.

Beading needles

These are longer and finer than ordinary needles and are available from most good craft and sewing suppliers. For some of the projects that use larger beads (and have correspondingly larger holes in the canvas), it may be possible to use ordinary needles, but I have listed beading needles throughout to be on the safe side.

Sewing thread

I prefer to use polyester sewing cotton as it is stronger and tends to 'slide' through the work easier. The mixed 'plaits' of thread are useful as you always have a choice of shades on hand to help you with extra colour changes.

Canvas

I always use double-thread canvas for beading. Polyester sewing cotton is obviously finer than tapestry yarn and it tends to get pulled tight into one intersection of single-thread canvas. Double-thread canvas stretches your stitch slightly and allows the bead to sit well on the centre of the stitch. The mesh of canvas you choose will depend on the size of beads to be used – the bigger the bead, the bigger the mesh.

Twelve-holes-to-inch is best for most embroidery beads (sizes eleven to nine) and probably results in the most classic, finest-looking work.

Ten-holes-to-inch means you can cover ground quicker, but you will need large (size eight) beads.

Six- to eight-holes-to-inch (rug canvas) is needed if you want to use the larger beads usually found in necklaces (⅙ inch/4 mm and up).

Preparing the canvas

For each project I have given the approximate area of canvas needed, including a 2-inch (5-cm) border. This seam allowance varies a little, depending on the individual stitcher, so do be generous. You need a good margin for ease of stretching and in case you want to alter the size of the background (for example, to fit your address book or jewellery roll). Zigzag-stitch round the edge of the canvas with a sewing machine to stop any fraying, or you can use masking tape instead. If you normally use a frame for needlepoint you might wish to use one for beading too, but it isn't necessary. You will find your canvas pulls out of shape far less than when worked with yarn and that it is, therefore, much easier to block when finished. I never use a frame.

Where to start

When in doubt, fold your canvas into quarters, find the centre point and work outwards from there. However, in many cases, I have suggested instead that you stitch in the basic outline of each shape which you can then fill in at random (for example, the animal outlines on the Peter Pan collar). Again, because your canvas will not get pulled out of shape in the way it does with needlepoint, you can be less conventional about the order of stitching.

How to start and finish a thread

You do this in a different way for beads and yarns.

For beads

You can knot the thread round the canvas, but make sure that the knot itself lies on the underside. Tie off the thread with a knot in the same way.

For yarns

Knot the first thread. Take the thread down from above the canvas at a point about 2 inches (5 cm) from the starting point. Once the thread is worked it will be secure and you can then snip off the knot. To finish, run the thread under a line of stitches at the back of the work. For subsequent threads, secure them by running each one under a line of stitches at the back of the work and bringing it through to the front where required.

The charts

Each square on the chart represents one bead or stitch worked over one intersection of canvas. Follow the charts exactly to establish your shapes, but you may wish to use them less rigidly to suggest colour. Or start by following them exactly and improvise more as your confidence grows. Add as many colours as you can.

The quantities

Beads can be bought by weight or string or container. As far as this book is concerned, 'one packet' means 1 ounce (25 grams), which is getting on for 1000 size-10 glass seed beads. However, the amount of beads that you get for weight varies enormously, depending on the size and quality of the beads. Mixed packets, which I have usually referred to as 'sweepings', because they are swept up and reclaimed at the end of each day, will also vary hugely. The number that you use of each colour also depends on the number of shades you gather and on how many of your own 'sweepings' you use. Usually you will only need one packet of each colour and size of bead and, in some cases, only a scant few. Look at the charts to see the proportions. Where you only need a few of the larger beads which can be bought individually, I have specified exactly how many you need.

The yarn quantities are also approximate as everyone stitches with their own tension. You may prefer to buy only part of the amount of yarn to start with and then you will be able to estimate how much more you need for yourself. I seldom worry about matching dye lots, even for backgrounds. If you blend in the new lot gradually, slight variations in colour are a plus.

To block your work

When blocking beadwork, I use a padded board and long steel pins. Place the work face down on the board and lightly spray the back of the canvas with clean water from a plant mister. Use a ruler to pin down one edge straight, sliding in the pins about ¼ inch (6 mm) apart. Use a set square to ensure your corner is at a right angle, then pin along the next side. Repeat this process until the canvas is secured all the way round. Leave to dry. You will need to re-pin and re-dampen the work a couple of times to make sure the canvas is fully stretched and has perfect right-angled corners. For those projects that have a greater proportion of yarn stitching, you may need to pull the canvas a bit harder and use tacks and a hammer. Make sure the work is completely dry before you remove it from the board.

Making your own designs

Take a photograph, buy a postcard or make a quick sketch of what you want to stitch. Alternatively you can trace around an outline if it is on your own hall tiles or living room curtains. Have the size altered, if necessary, using a photocopier. Use a lightbox to transfer the design on to canvas. You can set up a home-made lightbox by carefully balancing a sheet of glass between two chairs and placing a strong lamp underneath it. Place the design on the glass and cover it with your canvas. You will be able to see enough to mark your outlines on the canvas with a waterproof pen. Do try this method because, with a minimal amount of organization, you can stitch anything that takes your fancy.

Finishing techniques

Cushion pads

Place your canvaswork on a piece of featherproof fabric folded double and draw round it with a waterproof pen. Cut round this line, leaving an extra ½-inch (12-mm) seam allowance. Machine-stitch around the waterproof line, leaving a 3-inch (7.5-cm) gap, and trim the corners. Turn right sides out and press the seams. Fill with feathers collected from old pillows or use a commercial stuffing. Hand-stitch the gap to close it.

Cushions surrounded by a fabric border

Pin your canvaswork face up on your stretching board. Cover it with your border fabric, also face up, and pin them together at the corners. You will feel the raised area of canvaswork through the border fabric. Cut a hole in the fabric at least ½ inch (12 mm) smaller than the canvaswork. Turn under the edges of the border fabric and pin them to the edge of the canvas-

HOW TO TRANSFER A DESIGN ON TO CANVAS

Place the drawing on top of the glass and the canvas on top of the drawing.

Mark the design on the canvas with a waterproof pen. You can use the original as a guide when colouring the needlepoint stitches.

work. Gradually trim and clip the fabric where necessary to make it lie flat. Hand-sew in place. Cover the stitches with a fine cord.

Edging cords

Hand-sew the cord all round the work. To join the two ends, cut the cord leaving an extra 1½ inches (37 mm) at each end. Twist these two ends together and hide the ends inside the work, between the canvas and lining. Hand-stitch them in place.

STITCHES USED IN THE BOOK

Tent stitch
Tent stitch – right side. Work from left to right.

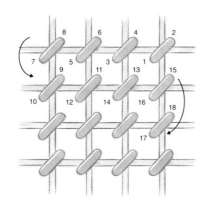

Cross stitch
This is worked over one thread of canvas, in the order shown by the numbers.

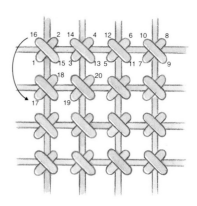

Tent stitch – reverse side.

Turkey work
Stitch the bottom row first and work upwards. Work from left to right only, which means ending your yarn at the end of every row. Use a strip of paper or a cotton bud to keep the loops even.

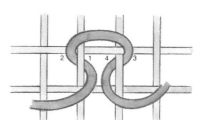

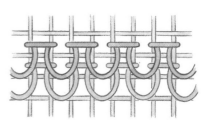

Diagonal long stitch
This is worked over two threads of canvas, in the order shown by the numbers.

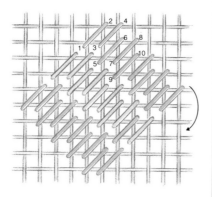

Straight long stitch
This is worked over two threads of canvas, in the order shown by the numbers.

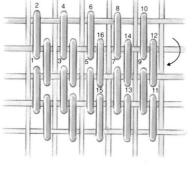

Random long stitch
This is worked both diagonally and straight as above, but the length of the stitches varies randomly in length, from over two threads to over three threads and over four.

Backstitch
Backstitch makes strong seams and can be used for finishing off a line of stitching.
  To work the stitch, make a small stitch backwards from left to right. Then make a stitch forward, of double length on the wrong side of the work so the needle emerges one stitch ahead of the first one.

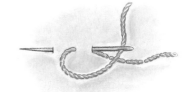

Mosaic stitch
This is worked over
one and two threads
of canvas, in the
order shown by the
numbers.

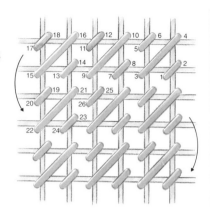

Couching
Lay several threads
of the same size.
Secure the end of
the couching
thread, then bring it
to the surface.
Secure the laid
threads with
couching stitches at
regular intervals,
as shown. To finish,
take the couching
thread to the back
of the work and
secure it.

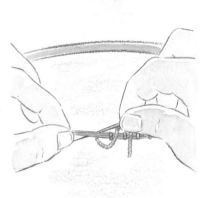

Bullion knots
The bullion knot is
worked by laying a
thread and wrapping
a yarn around it –
without penetrating
the canvas. Be sure
that the end of the
stitch is well-secured.
Pull the yarn tightly
and the stitch will
curl. When worked
loosely, this stitch
looks like curly hair.

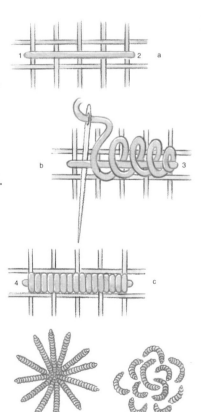

Smooth spider's web
Lay the spokes as
marked on the main
chart. Weave the
yarn into a spider's
web by going over
two spokes and back
under one, as shown
in the diagram.

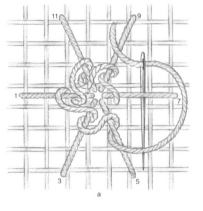

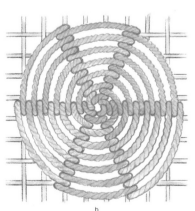

BEAD STOCKISTS

UNITED KINGDOM

Abington Handicrafts
140 Abington Avenue
Northampton NN1 4PD
Tel: 0604 33305

Barnyarns
Old Pitts Farm
Langrish
Petersfield
Hampshire GU32 1RQ
Tel: 0730 67201
(Mail order only)

The Bead Shop
43 Neal Street
Covent Garden
London WC2H 9PJ
Tel: 071 240 0931

The Bead Shop
21 Sydney Street
Brighton
East Sussex
Tel: 0273 675077

Beads Etcetera
26 St Govans Centre
Pembroke Dock
Dyfed

Botticelli Ltd
5a Crown Alley
Dublin

Campden Needlecraft Centre
High Street
Chipping Campden
Gloucestershire GL55 6AT
Tel: 0386 840583

Choices
10 Reading Road
Pangbourne
Reading RG8 7LY
Tel: 0734 844008

Craft Basics
9 Gillygate
York Y03 7EA
Tel: 0904 652840

Craft Frames
21 West Hill
Dartford
Kent DA1 2EL
Tel: 0322 278703

Craftworld
23-29 Queen Street
Belfast

Creative Beadcraft Ltd
Denmark Works
Sheepcote Dell Road
Beamond End
Nr Amersham
Buckinghamshire HP7 OPX
Tel: 0494 715606

Creativity
45 New Oxford Street
London WC1A 1BH
Tel: 071 240 2945

Els and Farrier
20 Beak Street
London W1
Tel: 071 629 9964
(Shop and mail order)

Glasgow Needlewoman
111 Candleriggs
Glasgow G1 1NP
Tel: 041 553 1933

Janet Coles Bead Emporium
128 Notting Hill Gate
London
W11 3QG
Tel: 071 727 8085

Janet Coles Bead Emporium
20 Reindeer Court
Worcester
Hereford and Worcester
Tel: 0905 616662

Janet Coles Beads Ltd
Perdiswell Cottage
Bilford Road
Worcester
Hereford and Worcester
WR3 8AQ
Tel: 0905 755888
(Mail order only)

Maple Textiles
188-190 Maple Road
Penge
London SE20 8HT
Tel: 081 778 8049

Michael Abakhan Ltd
Coast Road
Mostyn
Clwyd CH8 9DX
Tel: 0745 560312
(Telephone for information
about other branches)

Redburn Crafts
Squires Garden Centre
Halliford Road
Upper Halliford
Shepperton
Middlesex
TW17 8RU
Tel: 0932 788052

Treasures of the New Forest
The Coach House
Brockley Road
Brockenhurst
Hampshire SO42 7RR
Tel: 0590 23515

Voirrey Embroidery Centre
Brimstage Hall
Brimstage
Wirral L63 6JA
Tel: 051 342 3514

West Bow Needleart
94 West Bow
Edinburgh EH4 2JP
Tel: 031 220 0373

Wye Needlecraft
2 Royal Oak Place
Matlock Street
Bakewell
Derbyshire DE14 1EE
Tel: 0629 815198

UNITED STATES

Beadworks has the following
shops:

139 Washington Street
South Norwalk
CT 06854
Tel: 203-852-9194

905 South Anne Street
Baltimore
MD 21231
Tel: 410-732-2323

23 Church Street
Cambridge
Mass 02318
Tel: 617-868-9777

1420 Avenue K
Plano, Dallas
Texas 75074
Tel: 214-881-2117

68 Greenwich Avenue
Greenwich
CT 06830
Tel: 203-629-4500

349 Newbury Street
Boston
Mass 02115
Tel: 617-247-7227

225 South Street
Philadelphia
PA 19147
Tel: 215-413-2323

227 Goddard Row
Brickmarket
Newport
RI 02840
Tel: 401-846-1440

Stockyards Station
140 East Exchange Avenue
Fort Worth
Texas 76106
Tel: 817-625-2323

CANADA

Beadbox
1234 Robson Street
Vancouver
BC V6E 1C1
Tel: 604-684-2332

FRANCE

Le Comptoir des Perles
17 rue de la République
F-78100 Saint Germaine
en Laye
Tel: 39 73 40 51
(Mail order only)

GERMANY

Perlenmarkt have the
following shops:

Nordenstrasse 28
8000 München 40

Kaustrasse 93
1000 Berlin 12

Bohlenplatz 12
8520 Erlangen

Alte Gasse 14/16
6000 Frankfurt 1

Albrecht Dürer Strasse 16
8500 Nürnberg

Knopf & Perle
Kornhaus Platz 2
7900 Ulm

Perlplex
Guntramstrasse 58
7800 Freiburg

DENMARK

Panduro Hobby
Norre Voldgade 21
Copenhagen

BELGIUM

Crafts
Avenue Louis Lepoutre 45
B 1060 Brussels
Belgium

SOUTH AFRICA

Abacus
98 11th Avenue
Durban 4001
South Africa

JAPAN

Bijoux Bijoux
403 Ishiguro Buildings
3-15 Saiku-Cho
Shinjuku-ku-Tokyo
Japan

YARNS STOCKISTS

UNITED KINGDOM

DMC Creative World
Pullman Road
Wigston
Leicestershire LE18 2DY
Tel: 0533 811040

Paterna Wools
The Craft Collection Ltd
PO Box 1
Offet
West Yorkshire
Tel: 0924 811905

UNITED STATES

Appleton's yarns are
distributed in the US by:

Handwork Tapestries Inc
114B Allen Boulevard
Farmingdale NY 11735
Free toll: 1-800-645-9161
General information:
1-516-694-5276

DMC yarns are distributed in
the US by:

The DMC Corporation
Port Kearny
Building 10
South Kearny
New Jersey 07032
Tel: 201-589-0606

Paterna yarns are sold as
Paternayan in the US and
distributed by:

JCA Inc
35 Scales Lane
Townend
Massachussetts 01469

CONVERSION CHART

DMC	Anchor
307	289
310	403
352	9
367	216
368	214
413	401
420	374
420	375
420	888
433	358
433	371
437	362
437	368
444	291
444	297
445	288
504	875
550	101
552	99
552	100
552	107
606	334
606	335
666	46
676	3211
676	891
700	228
700	229
700	245
738	361
738	372
738	942
739	366
739	367
746	386
783	306
783	307
797	132
797	147
799	130
799	145
800	127
801	898
828	158
841	378
890	218
890	729
902	72
938	381
943	188
943	189
951	778
951	880
955	240
972	298
ecru	387
neige	2
blanc	1

PICTURE CREDITS

The author and publishers wish to thank the following sources for kind permission to reproduce photographs and illustrations:

Ace Photo Agency (Hans Schmied), 100 centre; Architectural Association (Hazel Cook), 93 bottom, (Richard McCabe) 94 bottom; Arnold Arnold 96; Ashmolean Museum, Oxford (copyright Mrs Eva Reichmann), 77 left and right; copyright BBC *Radio Times*, 29 left; Adrian Bentley, 34 bottom right; British Film Institute, 76; copyright British Museum, 39; Camera Press (Cecil Beaton), 50 top; Dean and Chapter of York (photographer: Peter Gibson), 16 left; Dickens House Museum, London, 29 right, 31 top right and bottom right; J. Alastair Duncan Ltd, New York, 80 top and bottom, 82-83; E.T. Archive (Historisches Museum der Stadt, Wien), 98; Mary Evans Picture Library, 34 bottom centre, 50 bottom, 68 centre; Sonia Halliday Photographs, 18, 58-59; Robert Harding Picture Library (Nick Servian), 100 top right; Michael Holford (Dickens House Museum, London), 30-31; Hulton Deutsch Collection, 34 top right; Mander and Mitchenson Theatre Collection, 34 bottom left, 70 top and bottom; Mansell Collection, 56 right; National Museums and Galleries on Merseyside (Lady Lever Art Gallery), 66 left and right; by courtesy of the National Portrait Gallery, London, 56 left, 60 right, 72, 75, 87; National Trust Photographic Library (Ian Shaw) 42 left, (copyright National Portrait Gallery, London) 44 top right, (Rupert Truman) 60 left, (Andreas von Einsiedel) 62, 63; City of Nottingham Museums (Newstead Abbey), 88-89, 89 right; Robert Opie Collection, 68 top right and left, bottom right and left; Panos Pictures (Penny Tweedie), 47; Photostage (Donald Cooper), 38; Rex Features Ltd, 26, 37, 52-53, 93 top; collection of Drs Martin and Judith Schwartz, 94 top; South Australian Museum, Adelaide, 48; from the book *Subway Ceramics* by Lee Stookey, Brattleboro, Vermont, 100 bottom; Topham Picture Source, 44 bottom right; David Wheatcroft, 23; Woodmansterne, 15 left and right.

AUTHOR'S ACKNOWLEDGEMENTS

The author would like to thank the following for their kind permission to reproduce their designs:

pp12-15 A panel from the famous Five Sisters Window, York Minster, which is a tapestry of silvery-grey glass known as 'grisaille'. Reproduced by kind permission of the Dean and Chapter of York.

pp16-19 One of the medieval quarries from a window in the Zouche Chapel of York Minster, depicting a wren chasing a spider. Reproduced by kind permission of the Dean and Chapter of York.

pp20-5 From an Amish pinwheel quilt. Indiana, 1930.

pp26-9 From gold tooling on a calf-bound book at the Dickens House, 48 Doughty Street, London WC1.

pp30-3 From the statue in Kensington Gardens, carved by Sir George Frampton.

pp34-9 From a Japanese watercolour by Toshusai Sharaku. The actor Segawa Tomisaburo as Yadorigi in a play performed in 1794. Copyright British Museum.

pp40-3 Inspired by the watercolour by Cecil Beaton (1904-1980) at Chartwell (National Trust and National Portrait Gallery).

pp44-7 From the picture by Marruwani *The Death of Purukparli* 1954 (Tiwi 1916-deceased) on display at South Australian Museum, Adelaide.

pp48-53 To be seen at the Tower of London.

pp54-7 From the Lewis Carroll Memorial Window in All Saints, Daresbury, Cheshire.

pp58-65 From the heraldic beast found in many forms at Knole, National Trust.

pp66-9 From a cabinet at the Lady Lever Art Gallery, Port Sunlight, England (National Museums and Galleries on Merseyside).

pp70-3 From the frock designed by Mrs Comyns Carr at the Ellen Terry Memorial Museum, Smallhythe, Kent (National Trust).

pp74-9 From the Max Beerbohm cartoon on display at the Ashmolean Museum, Oxford, by kind permission of Mrs Eva Reichmann.

pp80-5 From leaded Favrile glass. Tiffany Studios, New York c. 1900-1910.

pp86-91 From a detail of a bird on an inlaid table at Newstead Abbey, Nottinghamshire, England (City of Nottingham Museums).

pp92-5 From the White Cap Plate in the collection, and by kind permission, of Drs Martin and Judith Schwartz.

pp96-9 From an 18th-century game board in the collection, and by kind permission, of Arnold Arnold.

pp100-3 From an illustration in *Subway Ceramics* by Lee Stookey, Brattleboro, Vermont, USA.

The author would like to thank the following people:

For all their help with the source material:

Dorothy Lee and the Dean and Chapter of York Minster
Dr David Parker, Curator, Dickens House
Kate Alport, Curatorial Officer, South Australian Museum
The Vicar, All Saints, Daresbury
Lucy Wood, Curator, Lady Lever Collection
Mrs Eva Reichmann
Haidee Jackson, Assistant Keeper, Newstead Abbey
Drs Martin and Judith Schwartz
Arnold Arnold
Lee Stookey

To J. Floris Ltd of 89 Jermyn Street, London, for their kind help in supplying props for the photography on page 67. Established in 1730 and holders of two Royal Warrants, Floris is firmly established as an international brand with shops in Jermyn Street, Madison Avenue, New York, USA, Kobe in Japan and the Paragon Centre, Orchard Street, Singapore.

To Gina Rule for making up the nightdress case, the make-up box, the glasses case, the jewellery roll, the Alice band, the sponge bag, the book jacket, the toy bag and the clutch bag so beautifully.

To Sarah-Jane McClelland for making Daisy's frock and for all her help always.

To all at Anaya and the production team: Adrian Bentley, Roger Daniels, Rochelle Levy, Maggi McCormick, Carey Smith, Jane Struthers and my truly wonderful editor, Jane Donovan.

To Jon Stewart for his lovely photographs, and Steve Dew and Delia Elliman for their meticulous charts.

To Margaret Weare, Custodian, Smallhythe; the Aldwych Theatre and Nick Smith; Mr Bean at the Dickens House; Rosemary Kent at the National Trust; Fred Downer at Knole; for their patient help with location shots.

To Daisy Evans and Samson Jayes for modelling.

To Donald Newholm of Maple House Beads; Charlotte Smith and the Bead Shop; Tracey Els and Els and Farrier; Maria Dyaz and Jane Chamberlain at DMC Creative World Ltd and Jill Cooper at the Craft Collection (Paterna Wools) for their generous help.

And with love and thanks to Michael Clark, Tina Gray, Michael Jayes, Susannah Jayes, Martin Johns, Richard Leech, John May, Anthea Morton-Saner, Simon Needs, Diane Pearson, Anna Sheppard, Colin Wakefield, Claudia Zeff and Lisa Zeff, without whose help this book would not have emerged.

INDEX

GLOSSARY

The following terms may be unfamiliar to US readers:

UK	US
calico	unbleached muslin
coton perlé thread	pearl cotton
cushion pad	pillow form
featherproof fabric	firm fabric
matt (colour)	matte or flat finish
oversew	overcast or blindstitch
polyester sewing cotton	sewing thread
set square	carpenter's square
stranded cotton	6-strand floss
tack (in sewing)	baste
waistcoat	vest